·LOST·
CHURCHES
OF WALES & THE MARCHES

· L O S T ·
CHURCHES
OF WALES & THE MARCHES

PAUL R. DAVIS & SUSAN LLOYD-FERN

ALAN SUTTON

First published in the United Kingdom in 1990 by
Alan Sutton Publishing Limited · Phoenix Mill · Far Thrupp · Stroud · Gloucestershire

First published in the United States of America in 1991
Alan Sutton Publishing Inc · Wolfeboro Falls · NH 03896-0848

British Library Cataloguing in Publication Data
Davis, Paul R. *1962–*
Lost churches: Wales and the Marches.
1. Wales. Churches – Visitors' guides
I. Title   II. Lloyd-Fern, Susan
726.5

ISBN 0–86299–564–7

Library of Congress Cataloging in Publication Data
Davis, Paul R.
Lost churches of Wales and the Marches / Paul R. Davis & Susan Lloyd-Fern.
p.   cm.
ISBN 0–86299–564–7 $18.00
1. Wales – Antiquities – Guide-books. 2. Historic sites – Wales – Guide-books.
3. Borders of England (England) – Antiquities – Guide-books. 4. Historic sites –
England – Borders of England – Guide-books. 5. Churches – England – Borders of
England – guide-books. 6. Churches – Wales – Guide-books.
I. Lloyd-Fern, Susan, 1948–
II. Title.
DA737. D38   1991
914.204'859--dc20

Cover photographs: St Gwynno's church, Vaynor, Mid Glamorgan *and (inset)*
St Michael's church, Llanfihangel Abercywyn, Dyfed

Typesetting and origination by
Alan Sutton Publishing Limited.
Typeset in Sabon 11/14
Printed in Great Britain by
Dotesios Printers Limited.

CONTENTS

INTRODUCTION

'And some there be that have no memorial' – Apocrypha 44.9

There can be nothing quite so evocative to the eye as the sight of a ruin. Whether it be a mansion, castle or church, the skeletal remains beckon tantalizingly, inviting you to speculate on their dismal fate. Ruined churches in particular hold a special attraction: they provide a unique atmosphere, an air of mystery and veiled veneration. Overgrown with ivy and weeds, sadly neglected, they are the orphans of the past; the visible evidence serves only to enhance this loss. Buildings can, of course, be repaired, renovated and reinstated, but they are then rebuilt without the spirit of dedication which was the hallmark of the original founders. Perhaps it is this very sense of lost ideals and values that evokes the spirit within us when we gaze upon a derelict church.

From earliest times the parish church had always been a focal point for the local community and in many cases dominated the village layout. For the peasant population it was the institutional focus of business activities, and as such it acted as a meeting place as well as a place of worship. All kinds of decisions were taken at these meetings: decisions, for example, on who should, or should not, be allowed into the parish; or on what form of tithe would be acceptable to the community. In many cases the church would also be used to store valuable items such as grain or local produce, anything that could be accounted to the wealth of the community. The church was a sacred place, so it naturally made sense to use it for the benefit of all. If we can imagine a bank, village hall and church all rolled into one then we get some idea of the importance of the church to the medieval peasant.

So important was the church's place in medieval society that even in times of hardship or financial decline, each person within the community was obliged to contribute to its refurbishment and extension. But the medieval period was one of change: political, economic and climatic. The effects that this had on the peasant folk can be seen in the number of deserted medieval settlements throughout England and

Wales. It was during this period that many parish churches came to be abandoned. Before we look at the causes for the decline of the parish church, however, we must first try to understand the nature of the church in Wales and the Marches from its earliest beginnings.

HISTORY

Parish churches have always dominated the British landscape, providing us with one of the most tangible reminders of our past. Historical documentation about English parish churches does not become common until the later Middle Ages, but there is sufficient early written evidence to suggest that the parochial system in England, as we know it today, was evolving during the centuries prior to the Norman invasion (Ireland and Wales, and to a lesser extent Cornwall, comprised a Celtic Church and did not have a parochial system). Its origins are far from clear and are unlikely to be illuminated further, but it is acknowledged

The shrine-chapel of St Winifred at Holywell, Clwyd

that Christianity had taken root in Britain during the Roman period, although it had never achieved any great organizational status. Following the collapse of Roman power in the fifth century, and the subsequent incursions of pagan Saxon settlers, a rift developed between the western 'Celtic' churches of Wales and Cornwall. As a result their common tongue began to develop into two distinct languages, Cornish following more closely to Breton than Welsh.

Because of Wales' isolation the old pagan Celtic religions were never fully suppressed as in other parts of the country. This is evidenced today by the many holy wells in close proximity to chapels and churches. The water cults of the old gods were utilized in the new Christian religion to baptize members and to evoke 'miracle' cures. Very often the well or spring would be associated with an early saint, and a chapel would later be built on, or near, the holy site.

In Saxon England the new faith was reintroduced at the end of the sixth century by St Augustine and his followers, and centres of missionary activity were founded to spread the gospel throughout the land. The more successful the mission, the more it became necessary to establish outlying churches resulting in a network of smaller, dependent Christian centres.

It was during the period between the Roman withdrawal and the arrival of the Normans – the Dark Ages – that monasticism caught the imagination of the Welsh. Monasteries were often founded and endowed by ruling families, and often the sons of these tribal chieftains forsook the pleasures of the world for the austere, harsh, and contemplative life of a monk. From the ruling monasteries monks were despatched to convert pagans to Christianity. They established oratories, hermitages and chapels in outlying districts, and these early hermitages, in particular, were often the precursors of later chapels, some of which are mentioned in this book. The missionary-monks in Wales, to whom many of these early chapels are attributable, include St Illtud (*c.* 475–525), St Cadog (*c.* 450) and St Teilo (sixth century); but the most famous of all the early Christian Welsh saints must be David – Dewi Sant – who later became the patron saint of Wales.

The earliest church sites in Wales would have been no more than consecrated burial grounds for baptized members of the faith. Whether pagan or Christian, cemeteries were usually unenclosed, but during

Clynnog Fawr, Gwynedd. A late medieval church built on the site of St Beuno's Dark Age oratory

later centuries small burial grounds encircled by a wall or earthwork bank were constructed. Other than these surviving earthworks (which, without archaeological excavation, are indistinguishable from the smaller 'hill-forts' and enclosures built by the pre-Roman Iron Age tribes) only inscribed and carved memorial stones remain as material evidence for Christianity in Wales prior to the Norman conquest.

With so little left in the way of visible remains, it can be difficult to envisage these missionary settlements which served the religious needs of the lay people. Without documentation, most of the evidence is gleaned from excavations of early Christian sites. The original oratories and chapels were very small structures mainly built from perishable materials such as wood, or wattle and daub, and few have survived. Even some later stone buildings have, in the course of time, been razed to the ground.

In the light of this archaeological evidence, it would be reasonable to assume that, despite the building of these little churches, people still performed their acts of worship in the open air. The very first Christian ceremonies had been conducted in the open, by an itinerant priest or monk who had been sent out from one of the monasteries. Within a short time the sites where they chose to conduct their worship became permanently established, usually because new members of the faith chose to be buried there, and their graves would have been marked with a cross or inscribed stone. A small timber church was usually then built, with some form of enclosure, to set the place apart as a holy site.

Basically the churches which served the Welsh community were small, austere and primitive buildings, exhibiting none of the scale and grandeur of the Anglo-Saxon edifices which were appearing in England in the latter part of the Dark Ages. On the eve of the Norman conquest, England found herself in a much better position to withstand the unification by the Church of Rome that the invaders were about to impose. The changes that had been brought about by St Augustine's enforcement of Roman religious laws meant that England had over four centuries in which to adapt to the parochial system. Wales, however, had not been so fortunate; in AD 768 Bangor had become the first of the Welsh ecclesiastical communities to conform to the system sanctioned by Augustine, but other communities remained independent until well after 1066.

The Norman invasion brought the Celtic Church into line with the Church in England, and under the direct control of the Pope. Laws were enforced which marked the territorial boundaries of the Church into diocese and parish, an arrangement which has endured virtually unchanged to this day. Many of the old Celtic establishments were re-dedicated to saints and holy men more familiar to the conquerors, and their lands granted to the monastic orders which had been introduced from the continent, such as the Benedictines and Augustinians. The Cistercian order won greatest favour with the Welsh, for the hard working 'white monks' chose to set up monastic houses in deserted areas in the belief that they could turn them to profitable use. Desperate to curtail the power of those orders under Norman patronage, the native princes of Wales decided to champion the Cistercian cause by handsomely endowing monasteries like Strata Florida (Dyfed) and Margam (Glamorgan).

A greater effect the Norman invasion inflicted on Britain was the creation of the 'Marche', which meant boundary or mark, and territorially divided England from Wales. Of course, the Saxon king Offa had already set up a great earthwork dyke between the two races, but this would seem as nothing compared to what the Normans had in mind. After William the Conqueror had subdued the Saxons of England, he turned his attention to the constant menace of the war-like Welsh. Here in the Marches, where the rolling hills and gentle plains of the Midlands give way to the mountainous lands of the west, King William created the Marcher Lordships of Hereford, Chester and Shrewsbury, and placed in their charge the most trusted and rapacious of his followers. These noblemen had *carte blanche* to wrest, in whatever manner they chose, any lands from the Welsh and rule over them as virtual despots. The marches were to see much conflict in the centuries which followed, as is evidenced by the large number of ruined castles in this area.

Now that the churches had been officially brought under the control

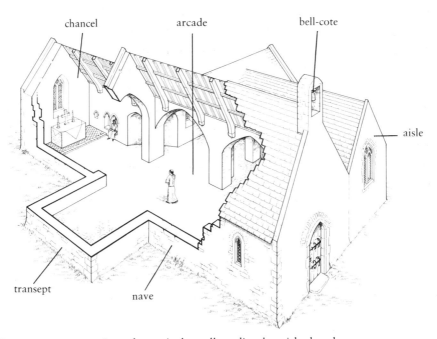

Cutaway reconstruction of a typical small medieval parish church

of the Roman Church, the Papacy had far more say in how they should
be administered. Once a suitable candidate had been found to act as
rector, for example, the approval of the bishop was needed before he
could be installed as spiritual leader of the community. The Church was
effectively taken out of the hands of the lay people, and their role in
church affairs would henceforth be as patrons. Moreover, many
patrons came not from the lay community, but from ecclesiastical
orders, such as the Knights Hospitallers. This organization of warrior-
monks had been formed to protect pilgrims on the hazardous route to
Jerusalem, and from their Welsh headquarters in Pembrokeshire they
took upon themselves the patronage of many churches in the area. They
also 'appropriated' churches. This was a formal process sanctioned by a
bishop, which gave the patron a portion of the church's income in
return for the maintenance and upkeep of the building – a responsibility
which was often sadly neglected.

Gradually, the role that ordinary people played in the daily life of the
church diminished as more and more of the wealthy and powerful
Orders took over the running of the parish church. Eventually the role
of the lay person was reduced to one of parishioner only.

This was the structure of the church system in Wales and the Marches
up to the second quarter of the sixteenth century, when Henry VIII's
break with Rome heralded the Reformation, and brought about a new
chapter in the religious history of the country. Whereas in England
there had been much anti-Papal feeling, particularly against a Catholic
Church grown rich with material wealth and political power, in Wales
the situation was generally the reverse. By comparison the Welsh
Church was extremely poor. There was not one Welsh speaking bishop
in the principality; in fact, most bishops were English and had little
interest in the affairs of the parishes for which they were responsible,
while many of the clergy were so illiterate that they were unable to
conduct the services in the proper manner. To many of the lay people of
Wales the Dissolution of the Monasteries in 1536–40 was an act of
total desecration. When the monasteries were stripped of financial
support, and pilgrimages to shrines discouraged, many of those
churches which had received monastic patronage fell into disuse. With
the advent of Protestantism, and the many diverse sects that it fathered,

the parish church was faced with the threat not only of decay, but also with the loss of what few parishioners were left, who sought a different kind of religious observance in the Methodist and Baptist faiths.

THE ROAD TO DESTRUCTION

It must not be imagined that all churches began their decline at the time of the Reformation; indeed the road to destruction had, for many, been traversed much earlier, while others survived up to this century only to meet with a similar fate. There are no hard and fast rules that dictate why some churches were abandoned while others flourished; each ruin has its own story to tell.

Of all the reasons for abandonment, it is plagues and famines which have most indelibly printed themselves on the popular imagination, while lesser, more persistent ills pass seemingly unnoticed. The Black Death of the fourteenth century did have a devastating effect on the population, particularly in England, where the great number of deserted villages attest to its severity. In Wales, alas, the records are fragmentary, so there is no way of being certain if the plague was indeed the cause of the widespread abandonment which occurred at this time. Rural areas of course were much less likely to contract the disease and tended to survive much better than their urban counterparts.

The weather was another important factor in the demise of villages and churches. The Gower settlements of Pennard, Penmaen (see p. 66) and Rhossili (p. 71) fell victim to the shifting coastal sands, and the vanished site of Hawton (p. 106) in Dyfed was overwhelmed by a freak tidal wave in the seventeenth century. It is apparent that the fate of many coastal settlements was dependent on the prevailing climate.

By contrast, the deserted village of Runston (see p. 10) in Gwent was deliberately allowed to fall into ruin, to rid the area of its vagabond squatters. Man can prove to be just as efficient a leveller as nature. The 'white monks' or Cistercians, despite their austere reputation, were also responsible for the ruthless acquisition and destruction of villages and churches. Many patrons donated gifts of land which could hardly be described as wildernesses of the type customarily taken in hand by the

Cistercians, and so great was their desire to hold on to these valuable gifts that the monks in effect created their own kind of wilderness: they evicted tenants, pulled down houses and took over parish churches. The twelfth-century cleric and chronicler, Gerald of Wales, provided graphic written evidence of the destruction taking place on the estates of the great abbeys in his *Speculum Ecclesiae*:

> All the monasteries in Wales are involved in one and the same vice . . . for they are wont to occupy the parish of mother and baptismal church, and either in large measure diminish their extent or obtain complete control over them, expelling the parishioners and leaving the churches empty and deserted.

According to Gerald the monks of the Margam grange of Llangewydd took the church from the parson and then proceeded to evict the parishioners. At night, upon instructions from superiors, they razed the church to the ground and carted away all building materials so that no trace would remain.

The profitable wool industry of the fourteenth and fifteenth centuries witnessed further population displacement as monastic granges were abandoned and the land given up to sheep grazing. The grange buildings were left derelict or were downgraded to secular farmsteads, and their chapels used either as places of private worship or turned into cowsheds or stables.

Another cause of ruination was warfare, and throughout the centuries Wales was never free from conflict. In over three hundred years of bitter strife and bloody conflict, from the Norman Conquest onwards, the fact that any churches remained intact is testimony to the faith and perseverance of the ordinary peasant folk. They had suffered greatly, having witnessed the wholesale destruction of their way of life and their villages reduced to wastelands.

The unproductive soil often forced the able-bodied to seek a better existence elsewhere; it was this particular aspect of the medieval period, rather than warfare or ecclesiastical machinations, which forced many small rural communities to dwindle and die. One question remains, which as yet historians are unable to answer, and that is why it was that some communities were able to ride these storms and keep something of their way of life intact, while others seemed to perish at the slightest hint of trouble.

St Kenya's church, Runston, provides sanctuary today more often for animals than for people

Population displacement was not just a medieval malaise: it is something that has affected rural areas up to the present day. In many cases, circumstances would cause a slight shift in a village's location, perhaps only a few miles away from its original siting, but the resultant changes could herald the death of the community. In such cases a replacement church would be built nearer the new settlement; a classic example can be seen at Llanfihangel Abercywyn (see p. 79) where the old church fell into disuse because of its remote location.

The upsurge in Protestantism, brought about by the Reformation, saw the loss of many of the larger religious houses and this dealt a crushing blow to the faith of many Welsh folk. The arrival of Methodism and the Baptist faith did much to alleviate the religious decline which had begun to take root. Religious services could be performed anywhere where there was a suitable meeting place. The large amounts of money necessary for the upkeep of a parish church were a drain on the meagre resources of the people, and so the less constrictive ways of the new mode of worship made economic sense. Wales was an exceptionally poor area of Britain and the abandonment of the parish church during the seventeenth and eighteenth centuries in favour of the Nonconformist religions should be viewed with little surprise. Many parish churches, now devoid of even the smallest amounts of financial contributions and ministering only to a faithful few, were slowly abandoned and fell into decay.

And so they have remained for centuries, their only parishioners stray animals, their only services ministering to the elements that prey upon their battered walls. Yet something special still remains; artists, poets and writers have all found a bitter tranquillity in their sorry plight. Inspiring architecture peeping from behind its leafy camouflage, a holy well with magical curative properties, a legend that turns fact into fiction; all these things and more await the inquisitive interloper and latter-day historical pilgrim.

DOES THE PAST HAVE A FUTURE?

The path to ruination can be likened to travelling down an imaginary road; on one side we have the parish churches and ecclesiastical buildings which are in use today and which form part of everyday life; while on the other are the ruined churches and chapels, the casualties of history and progress. Ruins are just as much a part of our environment as more well-preserved architectural structures from our past, and each successive generation will bear the heavy responsibility of creating new derelictions.

We cannot turn back the hands of time or hinder the advancements that new technology creates, nor should we, but we must inevitably reach a stage when we have to stop and consider just how much we are prepared to sacrifice. At present we are limited in our understanding of the development of oratories and our knowledge of these 'Dark Age' sites can only be increased by the wholesale excavation of those sites which are under threat as more land is given over to building and industrial developments.

The full scale investigations of Capel Maelog (see p. 116), in advance of building work, highlighted the enormous task which awaits the archaeologist. Other sites such as Highlight (see p. 34) and St Barruc's (see p. 32) have also been threatened by this kind of expansion of urban development.

This kind of ruination was not introduced with the twentieth century; it has been a continuing process over the centuries. Innumerable churches have been incorporated into farm buildings as rural communities waned, and the word of God was sought after in less grand, although more generally accessible, surroundings.

Other remains are mercifully spared, usually because they were encompassed within the confines of surviving religious buildings, for example the truncated churches at Llanidan (see p. 150), Abberley (p. 110) and Yazor (p. 132). The recent penchant for converting barns into expensive 'des-res' may very soon be extended to those medieval church remains which are substantial enough for conversion. Now disused Nonconformist chapels dating from a later period are already experiencing this new form of revival.

There are many sites which are even now under threat of being destroyed by the forces of nature. Llandanwg (Gwynedd) is a superb late medieval church which is slowly being buried beneath the sand, making the interior completely inaccessible. The scale of this problem is enormous and beyond the scope of even the most ardent conservationist.

And yet, we see amid the despondency of the situation a ray of hope. The rescuing of the ruined church of Llandeilo Tal-y-bont (see p. 62) proved to be more than just an exercise in preservation, for beneath the whitewashed walls was hidden a superb collection of medieval wall paintings.

Changing fashions can also dictate the fate of churches and chapels. On the foreshore of Rhos-on-Sea (Llandudno) stands the little chapel of St Trillo. Photographs taken earlier this century show a sad, roofless building, built from rounded beach boulders, the interior choked with rubble. But realization of the potential of this little chapel dawned on those with a vested interest in the town. On 16 June 1935, St Trillo's day, the chapel was re-consecrated and is now restored and open to the public every Friday at 8.00 a.m. for Holy Communion.

Likewise because of its magnificent coastal setting the chapel of St Govan (see p. 74) is a favourite tourist venue, and this has proved to be of benefit in keeping the chapel safe from further ruin. There are other superbly sited ruins mentioned in this book, and sadly it is not feasible to preserve all of them; indeed it would be foolish to expect a

Capel Trillo, a tiny seaside well-chapel

wholesale interest in ruined churches to be indulged and financed to the exclusion of other sites. Perhaps the least we can hope for is that they will be recorded and studied and their treasures removed and stored in suitable show places.

The medieval church was the only memorial that ordinary folk could leave as testimony to their existence, and surely it is our duty as their successors to preserve their legacy to us.

Mounton chapel in Dyfed served the large population of Narberth for several centuries; now it stands alone and uncared-for

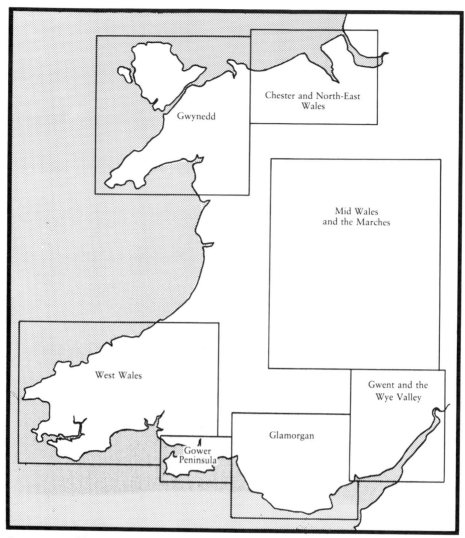

Gwynedd

Chester and North-East
Wales

Mid Wales
and the Marches

West Wales

Gwent and the
Wye Valley

Gower
Peninsula

Glamorgan

Areas covered by the gazetteer

GAZETTEER

Nearly a hundred lost churches in Wales and the Marches have been selected for inclusion in this gazeteer. The actual number of known sites is far greater, but such an exhaustive survey is beyond the scope of this book. We have, therefore, concentrated on the more important sites, those of some historical significance, or with substantial remains. Others may have a story to tell, either by unravelling the architectural mysteries of the building, or by recounting the strange and varied folk-tales which so often are integral with the real history of an ancient monument.

For the convenience of the visitor the gazetteer section has been divided into seven regions with location maps pinpointing the general position of each lost church. Further directions and access arrangements will be found at the end of each entry.

Many of the lost churches included here are freely accessible, while those on private property can usually be visited if permission from the landowner is first sought. But please follow the 'Country Code', and remember that these buildings, even in ruin, are religious sites and deserve the respect and care of all who visit them.

KEY

Key to site plans (unless otherwise indicated)

⌐ ⌐ ⌐ ⌐	site of walls
■	upstanding walls (earliest phase)
▓	additions (second phase)
▒	(third phase)
☐	(fourth phase)
⬚	(fifth phase)

Scale to site plans (unless otherwise indicated)

├─────────────┤	30 feet
├─────────────┤	9 metres

GWENT AND THE
WYE VALLEY

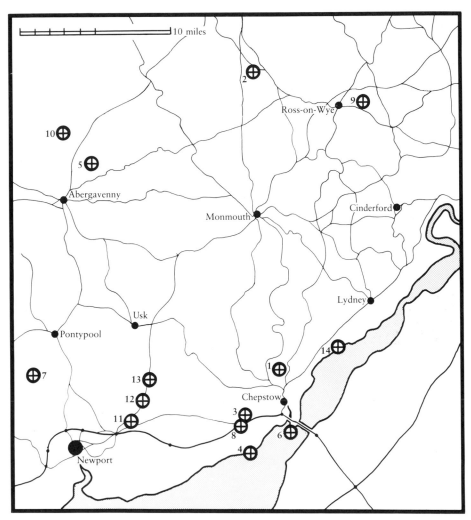

MAIN SITES

1. *St James's Church, Lancaut*
2. *St John's Church, Llanwarne*
3. *St Kenya's Church, Runston*
4. *Holy Trinity Church, Sudbrook*
5. *St Michael's Chapel, Ysgyryd Fawr*

LESSER SITES

6. *St Tecla's Chapel, Beachley*

7. *Llanderfel, Cwmbran*
8. *St Nyven's Chapel, Crick*
9. *Eccleswall Court Chapel*
10. *Stanton Chapel, Llanfihangel Crucorney*
11. *St Curig's Chapel, Cat's Ash*
12. *All Saints' Church, Kemeys Inferior*
13. *St Bartholomew's Chapel, Llantrisant*
14. *Woolaston Grange*

St James's Church, LANCAUT

(ST 536 965)

St James's church, Lancaut, is a Border church lost in the spectacular scenery of Wintour's Leap on the Wyndcliffe, within a loop of the river Wye. It is hardly noticeable that here the visitor is passing over the border from Wales into England, and in so doing, crossing a more visible boundary, that of Offa's Dyke. Lancaut may well be the smallest parish in England, with its half-dozen small farmhouses, yet here lie the remains of a Christian shrine which spans some twelve hundred years of Border tradition.

Originally this was a Celtic church, founded around AD 700 and dedicated to St Cerwydd, a holy Welshman of the Dark Ages, who has many other church dedications elsewhere beyond the Wye. It has been

The east end of St James's church, Lancaut

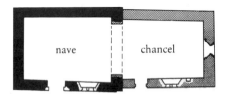

Plan of St James's, Lancaut

said that the western portion of the existing building was the original oratory, and the two small windows which can be seen high in the gable wall are features more characteristic of Anglo-Saxon architecture.

For centuries this small and simple building served the spiritual needs of the neighbouring serfs and bondsmen, but the sudden arrival of the Normans soon after 1066 brought changes. Only a mile or so downriver a powerful fortress (the first stone castle in Britain) was built at Chepstow, and the Welsh saint of Lancaut was ousted in favour of one more familiar to the invaders – St James. However, it was not until the later Middle Ages, when Lancaut was no longer a Welsh enclave, that this re-dedication was generally accepted. There is a theory that Lancaut had been leased in the tenth century to Welsh sailors exploiting the local timber trade from the Forest of Dean. The Domesday Book of 1086 records the traffic of the timber boats as *euntibus in silvam*, 'going into the wood', and tolls for the cargoes would have been paid at the new castle of Chepstow.

The church was still in use in the later Middle Ages, when it also served the needs of a community of lepers at a nearby 'hospital'. Local tradition claims that the village and church were decimated by a plague, but the silting-up of the river, and its effect on the local trade, could be a more mundane explanation for the slow demise of Lancaut.

Lancaut today is a forgotten huddle of farm buildings on a low hill sandwiched between the murky river Wye and towering limestone cliffs. A narrow, tree-lined lane leads to Lancaut, passing the over-grown earthworks of an Iron Age promontory hill-fort in the woods on the right. From the hilltop farmyard an unmarked footpath cuts across a field to the church, passing a number of stony hollows which are probably all that remains of the medieval dwellings. From out of the shadows of a woodland glade the bleached stonework of the church peers at the visitor, the effect heightened by the two small gable

Gable windows in the nave of St James's church, Lancaut, dating probably from the Saxon period

windows which resemble a pair of empty, haunted eyes. A south-facing doorway, the arch stones of which have only recently tumbled, leads into the small nave. The adjoining chancel is slightly larger in plan, and was probably built by the Normans in the late twelfth or early thirteenth century – in fact, the ornate round-headed east window is very similar to those in Chepstow Castle's Countess Tower, which was built soon after 1220. The square headed south window is a much later insertion. Out of the chancel oak and hazel saplings push their way heavenward without obstruction, for the roof has long succumbed to remorseless decay. The stone Saxon font was removed from Lancaut church many years ago and taken to Gloucester Cathedral, where it is now housed in the Lady Chapel. Surrounding the ruined church, and growing within the confines of the crumbling graveyard wall, are herbs and spices so often associated with the ancient healing arts. In particular, Elancampane grows here in abundance, its aromatic root complementing the aura of the venerable ruin.

Access:
Freely accessible. The remains lie in woodland beside the river Wye. From Chepstow follow the A48 for Tutshill and turn left at the crossroads along the B4228. After about 1½ miles a sharp turning left leads to Lancaut. Before entering the farmyard there is a gate on the left, and a poorly defined public footpath leads down the hill to the church.

St John's Church, LLANWARNE

(SO 505 281)

The old parish church of St John at Llanwarne is the largest and most substantial ruined church in Wales and the Marches. For size and extent of remains it surpasses the majestic ruin at Slebech in Dyfed (see p. 92) and, although it is denied the leafy covering and secluded setting of its western rival, its complex architectural history makes Llanwarne one of the most fascinating of all the sites included in this book.

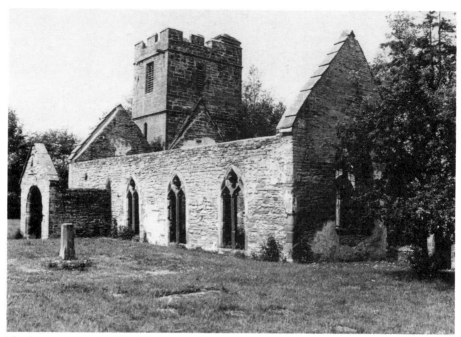

The imposing ruin of St John's church, Llanwarne, from the east

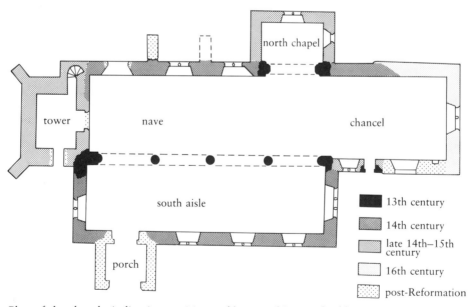

Plan of the church, indicating positions of later architectural additions

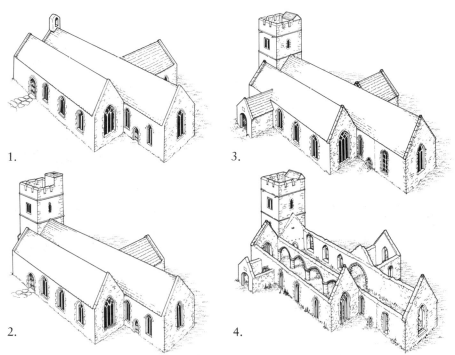

The development of St John's church, Llanwarne (note the gradual rising in ground level over the centuries). 1. Thirteenth century: a nave, chancel, north chapel and south aisle. 2. Fifteenth century: a tower has been added to the nave and the north chapel rebuilt. 3. Seventeenth – eighteenth century: a porch has been added, the chancel remodelled and the building re-roofed. 4. The site today

This noble ruin is sited next to the meandering Gamber brook, which flows through a small wooded valley not far from the border town of Ross-on-Wye. All the surrounding village houses, old and new, stand a respectable distance from the church, allowing it to draw the visitor's attention. Llanwarne has a splendour more usually associated with monastic sites; indeed, the first glimpse of St John's, nestling in the bend of the road, startles you into thinking that you have arrived at the site of a ruined abbey by mistake.

Llanwarne is an ancient parish. It is listed in the Domesday Book of 1086, but the *Book of Llandaf* records a seventh-century land grant wherein reference is made to *Lannguern* – 'the church by the alder trees' – a possible early name for this site. In the time of William the Conqueror Bishop Herwald 'consecrated Llaguern and in it ordained

The south chancel wall of St John's shows signs of many additions: the thirteenth-century door, a fourteenth-century window and, on the right, post-medieval additions are marked by a straight joint

Gulcet ap Asser, priest, and after him Simeon'. By 1291 the church of 'Llanwaran' and its revenues had been appropriated by the Augustinian Priory of Llanthony in Gwent.

It was during the thirteenth century that the simple Norman building was replaced by a grander edifice in the Early English style. There was a lengthy nave, with a south aisle separated off by an elegant arcade of four arches; an adjoining north chapel, and a chancel. Then, in the early years of the fourteenth century a substantial rebuilding programme was carried out, with some of the older walls being reconstructed. The reason for all this work was very likely due to extensive flooding, since there is hardly any difference between the level of the churchyard and the bed of the Gamber brook, which flows around the outside, and excavators believe this would have been the case in the fourteenth century also. Indeed, it is surprising that the church was built at all on this low-lying spot, and the flood-waters of the swollen river were to baptize the church more than once in its long history.

In 1405 a Papal 'Indulgence', in honour of St John of Bridlington, was promised to all who visited the church and contributed to its funds. A statue of the saint had been set up in the church, the cult having been introduced to the Welsh borders by the monks of Llanthony. The contributions were intended to finance further building work, and the main result of this money-spinning idea was the construction of the west tower: a tall, imposing example of late-medieval craftsmanship.

There were further minor additions and repairs during the post-Reformation period, the most obvious being those made in the seventeenth or eighteenth centuries: a new porch to the south aisle, and a large round-headed window in the chancel.

Over the years damp and periodic flooding was combated by the simple expedient of raising the floor levels. Needless to say, this did not solve the basic problem, and in the early 1860s further plans to restore the decaying building were rejected. Instead a new church of St John was built on a rise a little to the south, and the old site was unroofed and allowed to fall into decay. For over a century Llanwarne was left to the mercies of the weather and the creeping vegetation which took hold of the crumbling walls. The interior was often little more than a swamp.

In 1977 a local committee was formed to tidy up the ruin and make it safe for public viewing. At the same time the Department of the Environment carried out a detailed survey of the church, which enabled archaeologists to outline the historical development of the building. The clearing-up operation involved the removal of some gravestones to avoid the possibility of them being vandalized, although many such slabs had previously been built into the church walls, and used as window-sills! In the encircling churchyard can be seen the base of a fourteenth-century preaching cross, and the yard itself is entered through an attractive fifteenth-century timber-framed lych-gate. Altogether this is a most pleasing and atmospheric place, and one that is worthy of more public attention, for it deserves to remain as a monument to the tenacity and faith of our medieval forefathers.

Access:
Freely accessible. The church lies in the middle of Llanwarne village, about 7 miles south of Hereford. The way is clearly signposted off the A49 road to Ross-on-Wye.

St Kenya's Church, RUNSTON

(ST 495 916)

Runston lacks only a castle ruin to make it a textbook example of a deserted medieval village. Here, on a breezy hilltop with a magnificent view of the Severn estuary and Avon beyond, can be found the stony, scrubby foundations of no less than twenty-two houses; the site of a manor house; and a silted-up, disused road – all now overshadowed by the gaunt shell of a twelfth-century church.

To the untrained eye the ruined church alone appears to stand guard on the hill, but look closely at the undulating, stony ground, and the subtle patterns of the long-vanished settlement will appear, almost as if fossilized into the landscape. The overgrown road can be followed as it snakes past the hollows and earthworks marking the site of homes which once flanked the main street. Traces of the boundary enclosures can be made out at the rear of some properties. The buildings themselves would very likely have been of two types: solid stone

All that remains to mark this ancient village site is the ruin of St Kenya's church

A bird's-eye view of the church and village of Runston, as it might have appeared in the twelfth century

houses, and contrasting half-timbered structures, with roofs of turf, thatch, slate or shingle. Most of the village buildings were simple dwellings for the tenant and yeomen farmers who worked the nearby fields; some may have housed the workshops of important rural craftsmen, such as the blacksmith, weaver and woodworker. There may even have been a village inn, where the exhausted labourers could gather on a cold, wintry evening before a sputtering hearth, to talk about present problems and future hopes while drinking watery ale. Set back from the road, and with its own boundary, was the manor house; but despite the social standing of the occupants, the material comforts offered by the medieval building may not have been a great improvement on those afforded by the other dark, draughty and unhygienic dwellings in the village.

Dominating the spiritual life of the inhabitants of medieval Runston was the church. Even in ruins, some eight hundred years after it was built, it is still an impressive example of Norman architecture. The windows and chancel have plain, ponderous round arches faced with carefully shaped blocks of local sandstone. The tiny windows were little

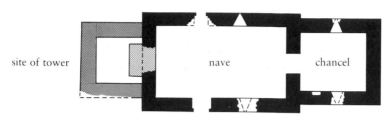

site of tower   nave   chancel

Plan of St Kenya's, Runston

more than unglazed holes in the walls, widely splayed on the inside to let in as much light as possible. They were never enlarged, nor was the blank wall above the altar ever used to house a more spacious window which would let light flood into the gloomy interior. The church has only a chancel and nave, and it is remarkable that the building was modified scarcely at all during its long history, apart from an attempt to construct a west tower. This ambitious project proved, however, to be beyond the means of the villagers, and a more modest bell-cote was substituted. The foundations of this failed architectural venture can be seen against the outer wall of the nave.

There are documentary references which suggest that the settlement was in existence by 1262; certainly the surviving fabric of the church is far older than this, dating from Norman times. By 1469 the village of 'Ronstoon' is specifically named, and just over a century later, thirteen tenants were recorded as holding land in the parish. Towards the end of the eighteenth century the decay had set in, and a map of 1772 indicates only six houses standing here. If we are to credit local tradition, the demise of Runston came when the few tenants struggling to continue living in the decaying village were deemed 'vagabonds', and their houses were either deliberately allowed to fall into ruin, or (perhaps more likely) were demolished, in order to drive out the undesirable residents. Such drastic action had taken place in many other parts of Britain, usually due to some rich landowner wishing to create extensions of his parkland, or to improve the view – at the expense of an established settlement. Whatever the reason for Runston's disintegration, the village earthworks and church now remain as a poignant and little-known memorial to a vanished medieval community.

Access:
Runston church is in the care of CADW: Welsh Historic Monuments, and is freely accessible. It lies on the right of a minor road from Crick to Shirenewton, off the A48, about 3 miles south-west of Chepstow. There is limited parking in a side lane, and a public footpath crosses a field to the church.

Holy Trinity Church, SUDBROOK

(ST 507 873)

A dreary little street beside a paper mill leads the way to the scant remains of Holy Trinity church, Sudbrook. The ruins stand perilously close to the edge of the glittering Severn estuary, at the rear of a row of terraced houses and within sight and sound of the Severn Tunnel pumping station. Modern industry is never far away here, and neither is domestic refuse, but perfection anywhere is a rare occurrence and visitors must take Sudbrook as it comes.

Just under two centuries ago, the traveller G.W. Manby was profoundly impressed by pre-industrial Sudbrook: 'Its retired situation, overshadowed by trees, produced peaceful meditation', he wrote, and he went on to pen a few maudlin lines about the 'gracefully mantled' ivy-covered ruin. Manby also included a lithograph of the church in his published travelogue, which shows an overgrown and roofless building comprising a chancel, nave and south porch, with a tall, double bell-cote over the central dividing wall.

Today, however, Holy Trinity church has lost much of its mantled splendour and most of the building has been reduced to a rubble-filled hollow within a railed-off enclosure. Miraculously the bell-cote and chancel arch survive to their full height (the lower half of the arch is Norman, the upper Early English). No less remarkable is the survival of the outer doorway of the porch; although the surrounding masonry has vanished, the dressed stone arch remains intact. Nothing, alas, survives – beyond archive references – of a Norman round-headed window

Only the entrance arch survives of the south porch of Holy Trinity church, Sudbrook

which formerly illuminated the nave, nor of a priest's door and piscina in the south chancel wall.

Having been extensively rebuilt in the fourteenth century by the De Southbrook lords of the manor, the church was abandoned in the middle of the eighteenth century. The last recorded burial there was of Blethyn Smith, a retired sea captain who died aged sixty in 1757. On his death-bed Smith requested that his body be consigned to the river, but he was dissuaded from this course by his well-meaning friends. The old sea dog commented sourly that in any case the church would soon end up in a watery grave. Time has proved Smith wrong, for the Severn has yet to claim Sudbrook church.

The surrounding graveyard has not been so fortunate. In the reign of Elizabeth I, the antiquarian William Camden described Sudbrook as lying 'so neare the sea, that the vicinity of so tyrannous a neighbour hath spoiled it of halfe the Church-yarde'.

Erosion has also removed part of the adjacent Iron Age fort, which was occupied by the native Silures tribe from the second century BC to the first century AD. Excavations at the fort in 1934–6 uncovered the foundations of medieval houses within the massive defences, which are perhaps the remains of a village associated with the early church.

Access:
Freely accessible, although the actual remains are fenced off. The church lies behind the Severn Tunnel pumping station, off the B4245, 1½ miles south-east of Caldicot.

St Michael's Chapel, YSGYRYD FAWR
(SO 334 184)

This is not the most easily accessible of sites: a lot of stamina is needed to climb the 300 metres from the valley floor to the ruins on the summit. The remains, alas, are not very exciting, but the accompanying view certainly makes up for this deficiency. St Michael's sits on the summit of Ysgyryd Fawr, a volcano-shaped mountain rising above the verdant Gavenny valley. A natural jagged crevice below the summit is said to have been ripped open by an earthquake at the time of the Crucifixion; perhaps not the most credible of folk legends, but Ysgyryd certainly has a mystical air about it, with its resemblance to Glastonbury Tor, which has no doubt inspired the more romantic traditions.

It is claimed that the soil of the mountain was brought either from the Holy Land, or from Ireland by St Patrick. Many years ago local farmers would carry away bags of 'holy' earth to scatter on their fields to ensure a good harvest. Ysgyryd soil was even placed inside coffins prior to burial. During the religious persecutions of the sixteenth century, Catholics are said to have gathered at night to celebrate Mass in secret on this bleak windswept mountain top.

Services were apparently held at the chapel as late as 1680, which implies that the building was still standing then; but by the nineteenth century only the legends and traditions, rather than archaeological remains, drew the attention of antiquarians. Today only a grassy hollow and some stony earthworks survive. These scant fragments outline a small, oblong building occupying the north side of a double enclosure which probably dates from the same time as the chapel, rather than indicating the remains of an Iron Age hill-fort, as has been suggested. Two dressed stone jambs mark the position of the entrance through which those devoted worshippers filed into the building on moonless nights to pray, hidden from the watchful eyes of those who would condemn them.

Access:
Ysgyryd Fawr is National Trust property and is freely accessible. Several footpaths climb to the summit from the surrounding lanes, including one which leaves the B4521 half a mile east of Llanddewi Court.

St Tecla's Chapel, BEACHLEY

(ST 548 901)

This little-known site lies within the shadow of the Severn Bridge, at a centuries-old crossing place of the great river. According to the Domesday Book, in AD 956 part of the Beachley peninsula was leased to 'Scipwealan', probably Welsh sailors, which implies that there was a small Welsh seaport here under English jurisdiction. This may explain why this important landing place was left outside the boundary of Offa's Dyke, which crosses the peninsula a short distance upstream. There are few traces of Dark Age activity to be found in this area, but St Tecla's chapel may have originated in this period, to serve the needs of the Welsh sailors and travellers using the Aust ferry. The remains are now very fragmentary and difficult to get to, since the tide has eroded the headland on which the chapel stood, and only at low water is there access to the island. Part of an archway, beside a modern lighthouse, can just be seen from the mainland.

Stories of encounters between famous people at this river crossing have become part of local history and folklore. In AD 602 St Augustine tried to have a meeting with Welsh clerics here, but as he remained seated the Welsh took umbrage at what they regarded as a lack of respect, and went off in a huff. A similar event nearly took place several centuries later, when another meeting was convened at this 'neutral' spot, between the Welsh ruler Gruffudd ap Llywelyn and the Saxon King Edward the Confessor. The parties remained encamped on either side of the river, unsure who should sail across first, for fear of losing face. In the end the pious Edward embarked for the potentially hostile Welsh territory, but as he neared the shore, Gruffudd, overcome by Edward's humility, waded into the water and carried the king across the shallow sea to his destination.

Access:
The chapel remains can be reached only at low tide, and local knowledge of the tide is essential. There is a good viewpoint of the island from Beachley Point beneath the Severn Bridge, at the end of the B4228 from Chepstow.

Llanderfel, CWMBRAN

(ST 264 953)

Situated on a hillside more than 300 metres above sea level, Llanderfel is one of the more remote sites. In the valley below, the industrial town of Cwmbran continues to expand, its new developments slowly creeping along the mountainsides and level river plain. Llanderfel, thankfully, remains aloof and unaffected by this modern progress. Only stony earthworks can be seen today (undergrowth permitting), but the scant remains have more than local significance. If we trust in tradition, then the chapel was founded here in the sixth century by Derfel Gadarn, Derfel 'The Strong', a veteran of the disastrous battle of Camlan in which Arthur and Mordred died. Leaving aside his military career, Derfel retired to this mountain spot to spend the rest of his days in more spiritual pursuits.

His humble chapel was no doubt venerated by local people, and with the foundation of nearby Llantarnam Abbey in the early twelfth century, the territorial rights formerly enjoyed by the Celtic establishment were acquired by this Cistercian house. Llanderfel may well have been the 'Old Abbey' referred to in a document of 1291, and the wily monks soon recognized the tourist potential of the mountain chapel and developed it as a place of pilgrimage. In the *Valor Ecclesiasticus* of 1535 the chapel was recorded as bringing in the modest revenue of just over £1 per annum. Llantarnam's other major upland property, Penrhys (see p. 55), was similarly developed, and indeed proved to be more popular and profitable.

All is now faded glory. The eroded and poorly preserved foundations of an L-shaped building can be traced, the main stem of the 'L' comprising the chapel itself, and the smaller right-angled section possibly a transept or an adjoining priest's house.

Access:
On private land. The almost totally neglected remains of the chapel lie in a field just west of a modern farm, beside a mountain track from Upper Cwmbran to Henllys.

St Nyven's Chapel, CRICK

(ST 490 903)

Crick is a photogenic cluster of medieval and modern houses clinging to a semblance of rural solitude in the shadow of the M4. The late-medieval manor now houses an archery centre and shop but was formerly the residence of the Moore family. In 1645 King Charles I dined here on his way into England via Raglan Castle, having been defeated at the battle of Naseby. There is a somewhat improbable story that as the fugitive monarch slipped through the back door of the house, the parliamentarian soldiers came in through the front!

Across the yard stand the remains of a small domestic chapel, no doubt the private place of worship of the lords of Crick Manor. This religious building is currently undergoing a transformation into a private dwelling. This is not the first time that Crick chapel, originally dedicated to St Nyven, has been put to a use conflicting with its original function. In the eighteenth century the disused building was turned into a barn, and two large doorways were knocked through the medieval

St Nyven's chapel has been transformed into a barn, but the remains of a medieval window can just be seen above the door

A cutaway reconstruction of St Nyven's chapel, Crick

walls, the central area being transformed into a threshing floor. A new roof was also added and the chancel windows were blocked up.

At first glance the chapel may seem indistinguishable from the surrounding farm buildings, but in the south wall can be seen the head of a trefoiled window, and the other windows retain their dressed stone frames. A few carved stones have also been re-used as jambs for the barn doors. A puzzling description of the chapel, published in *Archaeologia Cambrensis* (1909), mentions 'two square windows with a good rose window between' at the east end of the building; features which certainly do not remain today and never appear to have existed! The few surviving details suggest an early fourteenth-century date for this building, although a chapel was listed here among the properties of Llandaf Cathedral in 1119.

Access:
The chapel is privately owned and therefore not accessible to the public. However, it can be viewed from the roadside at Crick village, beside the A48 1 mile east of Caerwent.

Eccleswall Court Chapel

(SO 233 653)

The remains of this chapel lie within the confines of a private farmyard between Ross-on-Wye and Weston-under-Penyard. The latter village marks the site of the Roman town of 'Ariconium', once a flourishing centre of commercial activity with which Eccleswall had close connections. 'Eccles' is a place-name derived either from the Welsh *eglos* or the Latin *ecclesia* ('church'). Such a name nearly always denotes an ancient church site, probably pre-Anglo Saxon. If so then there may have been a church at Eccleswall when Ariconium was in its heyday. There is evidence that Saxon lords had a manor here, which was fortified in the Middle Ages by the addition of a motte and bailey castle. The eroded earthworks can still be seen behind the present farmhouse.

During the Middle Ages Eccleswall was a moderately important castle in the ownership of the wealthy and influential Talbot family, who either built or re-built the adjoining chapel and dedicated it to St Thomas the Martyr. The Talbots may also have replaced the old timber tower on the motte with a stone keep, for it is said that the ruins of such a building survived into the nineteenth century. The last known reference to the chapel is in a document of 1725 recording a land grant: 'Henry, Duke of Kent conveys to John Hal of Linton, yeoman, 30 acres in Eccleswall Manor formerly belonging to the Free Chapel'.

Today only the three-storey tower survives, its pointed roof rising above a sea of encroaching farm buildings. Above the entrance there is a stone carved with a knight's head; might this depict a member of the Talbot family? The few surviving remains of the chapel have long confused antiquarians. The Royal Commission on Ancient and Historical Monuments made no mention of the tower in their *Herefordshire Inventory*, except to call it a dovecot, and this opinion was also voiced by the architectural historian Sir Nikolaus Pevsner. Clearly the tower has at some recent time been converted into a columbarium, but there are no nesting holes in the inner walls and the remaining lancet windows would seem to proclaim its ecclesiastical origin. Another pointed window has been reset in the stable wall across the farmyard, clearly confirming the existence here of the lost chapel of St Thomas.

Access:
On private land but clearly visible from the roadside. The tower can be seen incorporated into farm buildings on the right-hand side of the B4224 Weston to Bromsash road, approximately 4 miles east of Ross-on-Wye.

Stanton Chapel, LLANFIHANGEL CRUCORNEY

(SO 311 213)

The mighty ruins of Llanthony Abbey, nestling in the Vale of Ewyas, draws many visitors every year to this part of the Gwent borderland. The lofty arches and towers of its long-departed monastic glories contrast with the war-worn shells of the many nearby Marcher strongholds. Both secular and ecclesiastical remains abound in the Marches, highlighting the two dominant aspects of the Norman invasion – defence and worship.

The route to Llanthony passes the medieval Skirrid Inn, and the twisted, leaning church at Cwmyoy (which looks as if it has had one-too-many at the inn!). No signpost points the way to Stanton chapel: although it was once the place of worship for the tenants of the adjacent monastic manor, it is now used as a cowshed.

Stanton was formerly the property of Llanthony, and although it

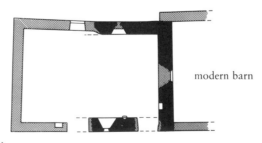

modern barn

Plan of Stanton chapel

The remains of the monastic chapel at Stanton have been incorporated into a modern cowshed

is recorded in local archives as being in existence by the fourteenth century, the surviving remains of the chapel appear to date from after 1400. The Reformation brought despoliation and destruction to the great abbey church further up the valley and, in common with other confiscated monastic estates, the manor passed into secular hands.

The few surviving details of the chapel indicate that it dates from the later medieval period – particularly the 'ogee', or double S-shaped heads of the dressed stone windows – but the building is far more complex than may at first appear. The earliest surviving masonry is embedded in a range of farm buildings. Inside the large barn one can see the blocked-up window which once illuminated the high altar. At around the turn of this century an upper floor was added, using carved beams which were probably taken from the adjacent seventeenth-century farmhouse. Then the entire western half of the building was rebuilt, as indicated by the plain roof beams and thinner walls.

This chapel clearly illustrates the value of making a detailed survey of any upstanding medieval building, in order to recover the history locked up in stone and mortar.

Access:
Stanton Farm lies just off the B4423 Llanthony road, 1 mile north-west of Llanfihangel Crucorney, near Abergavenny. A public footpath crosses the farmyard between the house and chapel, the latter identified by its ogee windows.

St Curig's Chapel, CAT'S ASH
(ST 372 907)

Curiously named Cat's Ash is a tiny hamlet along the back roads between Llanbedr and Caerleon, overlooking the broad river valley of the Usk. The winding lanes of the surrounding countryside have, by necessity, been supplanted by several broad ribbons of tarmac and concrete for the benefit of today's high-speed motorists. Such common-place engineering feats would not greatly have surprised the efficient, road-building Romans, whose major fortress, Isca (also called 'Caer-leon'), lay only a mile or so away on the meandering banks of the river. The modern A449 Llanwern to Usk trunk road brings the passing motorist to within a stone's throw of three ruined churches in the Usk valley. If intent on a visit, however, the tourist must forego the advantages of a good road to discover the joys of travelling along these twisting, hedged-in country lanes.

St Curig's chapel at Cat's Ash (where there was not a cat in sight throughout our visit!) is accessible enough, and although the remains are not open to the public, they can be seen from the roadside. It is the only survivor of several lost chapels in this area, and was listed in the medieval *Book of Llandaf* as '*capella Sancti Ciriaci*'. The chapel has also been tentatively identified as the '*capella de fraxino*' which Robert de Chandos granted to the Benedictine priory of Goldcliff in 1113. The few surviving architectural details, however, suggest a fourteenth-

St Curig's chapel, Cat's Ash, lies to the right of a seventeenth-century house; the outline of the blocked east window is clearly visible

century date for the building, and a reference in 1536 to the 'old chapel' suggests that it had become redundant by then.

The chapel has survived to this day comparatively intact, though not without some modifications. The north wall has been removed and an upper floor inserted, while the interior is now used as a garage and storeroom. The tall east gable, its window blocked, can be seen from the roadside, but the rest of the chapel has been virtually submerged by later buildings – on the west by a range of modern farm buildings and on the south side by a post-Reformation house, with a date plaque of 1604 above the doorway.

Access:
St Curig's chapel lies on the right-hand side of a minor road from Christchurch (Caerleon) to Llanbedr, just off the A48 at Llanwern.

All Saints' Church, KEMEYS INFERIOR
(ST 382 927)

Leaving the carefully manicured environs of St Curig's chapel, we now move on towards Usk where, in a secluded riverside grove opposite sixteenth-century Kemeys House, will be found the remains of All Saints' parish church. A visit here in winter or spring is recommended, for once the growing season is in full swing all that can be seen are the rounded tops of gravestones rising above the surface of a green sea of nettles and bracken.

Some of the old foundations can just be made out, but most of the site has been engulfed in a leafy shroud. Behind a curtain of foliage on the chancel wall is a modern plaque which commemorates the demolition of All Saints' by the Church authorities in 1960–62. The neglected building had become so unsafe that it was decided to raze it to within a few feet of ground level, and to use the stones for building the new east end of Newport cathedral. 'The place whereon thou standest is Holy ground', the plaque reminds us; a worthy sentiment, ignored by the rapacious undergrowth.

The building itself comprised a chancel, nave and south porch, with additional doors in the west and south-east walls. Where the nettles allow a close examination of the crumbling stonework a straight, vertical joint will be seen between the nave and chancel walls, indicating that the latter is an addition, or the result of rebuilding. The details visible prior to demolition suggested a fifteenth-century date, but a church here is mentioned in a document of *c.* 1314, and the west entrance had a round-headed Norman doorway.

In the solitude of this woodland setting the gravestones are poignant reminders of our mortality. There is an eighteenth-century memorial to 11-year-old Thomas William, 'drowned in the river Usk', and another to the wife of Revd Price, who was laid to rest 'In God's store-house beneath this slab'. Several inscriptions to children who never saw their second birthday serve to remind us of an age when infant mortality was a common occurrence.

Access:
A short distance beyond St Curig's chapel a left-hand turn signposted

to Llantrisant leads past Kemeys House and under the A449 Usk road. Just past the flyover is a lay-by, and an unmarked path leads back from here alongside the A449 to All Saints', which lies about ¼ mile along the track.

St Bartholomew's Chapel, LLANTRISANT

(ST 393 948)

A short distance further along the road is the third, and sadly the most ruined, of the lost churches in the Usk valley. It is not known for certain when St Bartholomew's was abandoned, but it appears to have remained in ecclesiastical use until the eighteenth century, when it was converted into a cowshed. It retained this humble function into this century, until at last the roof fell in and the walls collapsed. Only a short length of stonework survives above ground, and the chapel's remains appear to be in danger of disappearing altogether. It's an undignified – but familiar – end for such a distinguished building; the elaborately decorated gable windows (recorded in drawings and photographs made earlier this century by the Royal Commission on Ancient and Historical Monuments) are a particularly sad loss.

Access:
St Bartholomew's lies about 1 mile further along the road from All Saints. Turn right past White Hall Farm, and then right again towards Bertholey House. The remains lie in a field on the left.

Woolaston Grange

(ST 588 983)

The manor of Woolaston was in existence long before the Normans arrived in England, and at the time of the conquest it belonged to Britric, son of Alfgar. After the conquest William I granted the manor to his loyal follower and kinsman, William Fitz Osbern, the builder of nearby Chepstow Castle. A later owner, Walter de Clare, founded the Cistercian abbey at Tintern, and gave the manor to the monks in 1131. The monastic labourers, or lay-brothers, worked the manor as a grange or farm, and their spiritual needs were served by a small chapel. In the 1700s this chapel was used as a malthouse, and in 1921 it was converted into a two-storey granary. The chapel was still recognizable in the 1940s when it formed the east end of a range of farm buildings. It retained its bell-cote, two lancet windows in the north wall, and a window at the eastern end above the altar, the form of which suggests that the building dates from the thirteenth century.

Sadly, much of the building was demolished in the 1960s due to the fact that the roof had collapsed, rendering the rest of the chapel unsafe. Only part of the west wall remains and this appears to date from the time of its conversion into a malthouse.

Access:
The scant remains lie on private land on the banks of the Severn, at Woolaston Grange farm, off the A48 between Chepstow and Lydney.

GLAMORGAN

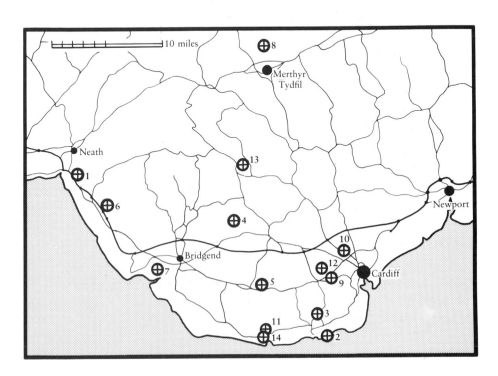

MAIN SITES

1. *St Baglan's Church, Baglan*
2. *St Barruc's Chapel, Barry Island*
3. *Highlight, Barry*
4. *St Peter's Church, Llanbad*
5. *St James's Chapel, Llanquian*
6. *Hen Eglwys, Margam*
7. *St Roque's Chapel, Merthyr Mawr*
8. *St Gwynno's Church, Vaynor*

LESSER SITES

9. *St Mary's Church, Caerau*
10. *St Mary's Church, Cardiff*
11. *East Orchard, St Athan*
12. *St Fagan's Chapel, St Fagans*
13. *Upland Chapels: Penrhys*
14. *West Aberthaw Chapel*

St Baglan's Church, BAGLAN

(SS 753 923)

Like many Welsh churches the origins of the monastic centre at Baglan are lost in the mists of the Dark Ages. According to tradition, Baglan was the son of a Breton prince and was educated at St Illtud's college, Llantwit. On leaving, Illtud presented Baglan with a crozier-staff as a gift, and told him to seek 'a tree that bore three sorts of fruit, and there erect a church'. Baglan travelled far and wide before he arrived at a narrow wooded valley by the coast, where he saw a tree that had a litter of pigs at the roots, a beehive in the hollow trunk, and a crow's nest in the branches. However, the saint disliked the sloping hillside location and started to build his church on the coastal plain below, but every night the foundations were mysteriously moved to the pre-ordained spot until Baglan acquiesced and built his shrine where it now stands. This was propitious, for today St Baglan's church is safely out of the way of the steel-works and housing estates which have engulfed the coastal plain over the last century.

The surviving late-medieval building is a far cry from the early church raised by Baglan, and all that remains of the pre-Norman establishment is a ninth- or tenth-century cross-stone decorated with Celtic knotwork and bearing the name 'Brancu'. But as late as 1700 Baglan's wonder-working crozier survived here, and was believed to be 'a sacred relick which had wonderfull effects on the sick'. A local antiquarian, writing in *c.* 1690, also noted that the church was held by the local inhabitants to be 'more than ordinary sacred'. Alas, little of this awe and mystery remains to be experienced today. In 1882 a new church was built nearby to replace the old, cramped parish church, and

Plan of St Baglan's   blocked doorway

after the Second World War the rural surroundings were irreparably changed with the arrival of modern industrial activity and the ensuing need for extra housing. Photographs taken earlier this century show the plain, homely interior cluttered with box pews and a crumbling plaster ceiling.

Although in serious decay, the old church remained in use until a disastrous conflagration reduced the building to a gutted shell. It is now an echoing ruin, with insecure walls, filled-in windows and a tottering, top-heavy bell-cote above the west door. This doorway has a round-headed arch, suggesting a twelfth-century date for the western end of the church, but all the other surviving carved stones indicate a late-medieval rebuilding. Grinning faces adorn the sides of the Perpendicular window in the chancel wall, while beside it can be traced the outline of a blocked south door.

In the graveyard below the church are several tombs of interest. There is a stumpy cross-stone marking the grave of an eleventh-century dignitary, and there are also two memorials to members of the Blaen Baglan family, dated 1662 and 1681. The armorial bearings include three chevrons, denoting descent from Iestyn ap Gwrgant, the Welsh lord of Glamorgan during the Norman invasion. Gwrgant's descendants, the lords of Afan, threw in their lot with the conquerors, styled themselves 'de Avene' and founded a Norman-type borough and castle at nearby Port Talbot. Their original Welsh stronghold, 'Plas Baglan', can be found in the woods across from the church.

It was once planned to remove the old parish church to the Welsh Folk Museum at St Fagans, but this project was abandoned – perhaps wisely, considering the supernatural building problems St Baglan encountered here all those centuries ago!

Access:
Freely accessible, since the ruin lies within the upper churchyard of the new parish church. Baglan lies just off the M4 at junction 42, 1½ miles north-west of Port Talbot.

St Barruc's Chapel, BARRY ISLAND
(ST 119 665)

St Barruc's importance – as one of the few excavated chapels known to have contained the relics of an early Christian saint – is belied by the incongruity of its setting. An on-site information plaque provides an historical summary of the building, but visitors must peer at the stony foundations and shattered walls through a high barbed-wire fence, for the chapel is situated at the rear of a former Butlins' holiday camp! Despite the great popularity of Barry Island as a holiday resort, there are probably few visitors who may know of the existence of this important and complex historical site.

Of course, St Barruc can hardly be blamed for setting up his hermitage on a tidal island that was to become the biggest summer tourist venue in Glamorgan. Even as late as 1890 Barry Island was an untamed wilderness of heath and warren, but with the establishment of

St Barruc's: a suggested reconstruction of the chapel and priest's house as they stood during the fourteenth century

the nearby docks, and the building of the causeway which links the island with the mainland by road and railway at the end of the last century, the island was opened for commercial development. In 1895 the curator of the Cardiff Museum, John Storrie, undertook excavation of archaeological sites threatened by development. St Barruc's chapel was among the sites he studied, which also included prehistoric burial mounds, ruined medieval buildings and two holy wells. (A few of the mounds still survive on the headland of Friar's Point.) Re-excavation of the chapel in 1967–8 greatly increased our understanding of the remains. (A full account of the excavations at this site will be found in *Transactions of the Cardiff Naturalists' Society*, vol. XCIX (1981).)

The earliest surviving masonry dates to the twelfth century, although the surrounding land had been held in reverence for long before that, since a number of slab-lined graves of early Christian type were discovered beneath the floor and walls of the humble Norman building. This building originally consisted of a simple nave with an 'apsidal' or rounded chancel – an uncommon feature of Welsh churches, although another Glamorgan island church, Burry Holms in Gower (see p. 59) had a similar structure. This modest stone church was transformed in the fourteenth century, no doubt as a result of the increased wealth brought to the area by pilgrims to the shrine of St Barruc. Piecemeal rebuilding altered the overall appearance of the chapel when a large porch and a more typical square-ended chancel were constructed. A dwelling-house for the attendant priest was also built, the inner room of which abutted against the outer wall of the chancel, and this led Storrie to suggest that there may have been a 'squint' or peep-hole in the wall to enable the resident priest to keep a watchful eye on the altar-side shrine.

A short distance away from the chapel stood a holy well dedicated to the saint. The trickling waters were believed to cure a variety of illnesses, and it was common practice for visitors to throw in a bent pin as a votive offering after drinking the healing waters. (This tradition, which has its roots in pre-Roman times, is continued today in a less serious manner when people throw coins into fountains or ornamental wells 'for good luck'.) When John Storrie cleared out St Barruc's well he found numerous bent pins which testify to the former renown of the well, and the tenacity of pagan traditions in a Christian environment.

The twelfth-century cleric and raconteur Gerald of Wales had a particular affection for Barry, since his family came from there, and the scant remains of their castle can be seen on the hill above the modern town. Gerald recounted the story of a strange rock on the shore of the island from which, if you pressed your ear against it, the sounds 'of blacksmiths at work, the blowing of bellows, the strokes of hammers, and the harsh grinding of files on metal' could be heard. He reasoned that the noise could be that of the sea rushing into clefts in the rock, but added that the strange sounds could be heard even at low tide. Gerald was also the first traveller to record the 'ivy clad chapel' on the island, where the mortal remains of the Irish saint lay enshrined. Around 1540 the indefatigable Tudor antiquarian, John Leland, noted the 'fair little chapel of S. Barrock, wher much Pilgrimage was'; a comment on the disastrous effect the Reformation was having on the local tourist industry! After Leland's time the neglected chapel became a victim of the shifting sands, with only the warren rabbits for pilgrims.

Access:
The chapel lies near the highest point of Friar's Road, uphill from the railway station on Barry Island, which lies 7 miles south-west of Cardiff.

Highlight, BARRY
(ST 707 698)

The present-day building craze has brought a modern housing estate to within a perilously close distance of the ruined church and deserted medieval village of Highlight. The curious name is, in fact, due to a misreading of the older Welsh place-name 'Uchelolau', meaning 'the high road', a reference to the deeply-rutted lane which passes the site of the village, and which may have been in use long before the Normans arrived in Wales.

It is this 'road' that the visitor must use to reach the old parish church, of which all that now remain are the restored foundations of the chancel and nave, exposed during excavations by the Barry and

Vale Archaeological Group between 1964 and 1969. These excavations concentrated not only on the church, but also on two medieval house-sites, a corn-drying kiln and a moated manor house which is of twelfth- to fifteenth-century date.

Highlight was a manor of the lordship of Dinas Powys, and was held by the De Sumeri family from the early days of the Norman conquest of Glamorgan. Their modest dwelling continued in use until the fifteenth century when the new lords of the manor, the St John family, built a more substantial hall nearby. This has been incorporated into an outbuilding of the existing eighteenth-century Highlight Farm.

At the beginning of the thirteenth century a tiny stone church was built at Highlight for the use of the villagers, and this was incorporated as the chancel during later rebuilding; straight joints in the masonry indicate that the nave was also added later. Finds from the excavations made during the 1960s revealed that the building was finer than the scant ruins would suggest: the roof was slated and capped with scalloped ridge-tiles; there were two altars, one in the usual position against the east wall, and another in the north-east corner of the nave. The inner walls were plastered and painted. Many burials were discovered beneath the floor of the church, including that of a priest interred in a wooden coffin along with two pewter chalices and a paten. One of the last recorded burials to take place here – that of William St John – was in December 1563, soon after which the church was abandoned.

The graveyard is now a green field, with not a headstone in sight, and only the low walls of the church itself remain above ground. Little too can be seen of the rest of Uchelolau village. Finds of iron slag, hearths

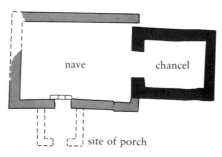

Plan of Highlight, Barry

The excavated walls at Highlight mark the site of this chapel and deserted village

and potsherds indicate that most of the houses were arranged alongside the main road. What is now a muddy track flanked by weeds and bushes was once the busy thoroughfare of this lost hamlet. On the north-east side of the churchyard boundary stood a two-room house, possibly the dwelling of the attendant priest. The inner room was warmed by a hearth, but the presence of a sump and drain in the floor of the outer chamber suggests that rising damp was at least one of the problems that the occupant of this humble dwelling had to contend with.

Access:
Freely accessible. The ruins lie in a field beside a public footpath from Highlight Farm to Northcliff, 1 1/2 miles north-west of Barry. A waymarked path can be followed from opposite Colcot school on the A226.

St Peter's Church, LLANBAD

(SS 993 853)

Llanbad is the silent sentinel of the Glamorgan uplands. A forlorn, remote ruin huddled in a fold of hills on the edge of the *Blaenau*. To the south stretches an uninterrupted view over the Vale of Glamorgan to the narrow, glittering ribbon of the Bristol Channel and the distant hills of Exmoor and the Quantocks. Turn around and you face the rising heights of the coalfields, dissected by narrow winding valleys scarred by a century or more of 'black-gold' mining. On a fine clear day the bracing climb to lofty Llanbad can be an exhilarating and breathtaking way to spend an afternoon, but in the bleak grip of the often inclement and unpredictable Welsh weather the picture can be very different. It's also sad to say that the needs of the electricity network have not always taken account of aesthetic considerations, and the landscape to the east is marred by a row of pylons marching across the mountainside.

St Peter's church (Llanbedr-ar-fynydd) is now a ragged ruin, with walls varying from knee-high to more than head-high. An equally ruinous drystone wall marks the churchyard boundary. All the dressed stones have long been stolen, and the building's outline on its own can only indicate a thirteenth- or fourteenth-century date, with a chancel and south porch being additions to the earlier nave.

The church was last used regularly in 1812, but as late as the 1960s

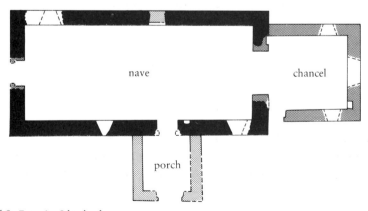

Plan of St Peter's, Llanbad

A distant view of the remote, mountain-top site of St Peter's church, Llanbad

services were held once a year in the roofless shell. A photograph taken earlier this century shows the building fairly intact, engulfed in a luxuriant grove of Scots Pine. Decay swiftly set in, and the ruins now stand stark and bare on the hilltop. There were many old gravestones in the churchyard, but the few survivors lie broken and scattered about the mountainside.

Here lieth the Body of
Mary Robert Daughter of
David Robert of this Parish
who died August 1775 aged 29 years

Poor David had buried his 32-year-old son only the previous March, although he himself lived on into the nineteenth century, as we discover from the inscription on another discarded memorial slab.

The eighteenth century was a particularly vibrant period for Llanbad. Its remote and romantic setting made it a popular location for marriages, and the parish records reveal that there were more weddings solemnized here than at the mother church of Coychurch in the vale below. At the beginning of that century a local antiquarian described Llanbad as a 'Chappel of Ease, a ruinous thing till of late yeares it was rebuilt by ye advice and consent of ye vestr, whose best relations lived there and granted them prayers once a Sunday'. The unsophisticated lifestyle and habits of the parishioners caused problems for the Church authorities; in 1731 some Cowbridge tradesmen were fined 6d. each for 'selling ale, gingerbread, and cakes' on a Sunday, and during the *Gwyl Mabsant* festivities on St David's Day, Llanbad was the scene of a riotous gathering of local people dancing, drinking, fighting and gambling in celebration of the returning spring. Such activities inevitably aroused the ire of Methodist preachers, and their repression of such high spirits led eventually to the neglect and abandonment of this remote church.

Even today Llanbad remains a centre of controversy, since there is a strong belief held by some researchers that this is the burial site of King Arthur: a large slab, which is claimed to have been the legendary king's tombstone, has been removed from the chancel floor. Plans are in hand to carry out a scientific excavation of the church, but until such time

Llanbad's claim, like that of so many other sites which declare an Arthurian connection, must be regarded with a certain amount of scepticism. Llanbad may well be a fitting resting place for a Dark Age folk-hero, but on the distant horizon the hump of Glastonbury Tor – legendary Avalon – also beckons all dedicated Arthurian pilgrims.

Access:
The church can be reached from a waymarked ridgeway footpath along Mynydd y Gaer. Several paths lead up to Llanbad from Brynna and Llanharan in the south (off the A473) or Glynogwr and Thomastown in the north (off the A4093).

St James's Chapel, LLANQUIAN
(ST 018 744)

Little-known Llanquian is not one of the most easily recognizable of sites. The heavily-disguised building forms part of a sprawling seventeenth- and eighteenth-century farmstead on the east side of Stalling Down, in the Vale of Glamorgan. Indeed, it might easily be mistaken for part of the decaying farm outbuildings (it is now used as a stable and hay store), and only recently has it been identified as the 'lost' chapel of St James.

A religious building at Llanquian has long been known. In a twelfth-century charter of properties held by Tewkesbury Abbey reference is made to the *Capella St Jacobi de Landcoman*, and until the last century part of the Holy Cross church, Cowbridge, was known as the 'Llanquian Aisle' and served the needs of the parishioners who had formerly worshipped at the little hillside chapel.

As none of the farmstead buildings showed any outward signs of having been a medieval chapel, it was assumed that St James' had long been destroyed. However, fieldwork by the Royal Commission on Ancient and Historical Monuments revealed that part of the outbuildings incorporated the elusive chapel. Although the ecclesiastical origin of the remains is not immediately obvious, for the observant

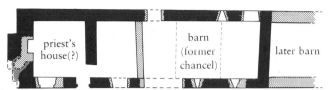

Plan of St James's, Llanquian

visitor some architectural details hint at the antiquity and significance of this building. In the eighteenth century the derelict chapel was converted into a house, adding to its present-day disguise. Although conversion into a house is not an uncommon fate for redundant churches, Llanquian is unusual in that it also had an apparently contemporary dwelling integrated into the west end of the nave, perhaps for use by the attendant priest.

The old chapel is marked by a tall, slender chimney stack which rises from the gable wall above a tangle of undergrowth and disused farm machinery. The interior has been partitioned off and an upper floor inserted, but much of the chapel is unobscured, and the modern corrugated metal roof is held up by three carved medieval beams. Beyond the crumbling building the hillside slopes down to a steep-sided ridge, crowned by the earthworks of Nerber Castle, the stronghold of the manor of Llanquian. Tumbled stone walls and the shell of a small tower are all that survive of this thirteenth-century fortified residence of the De Nerber family. Less obtrusive than either the chapel or castle are the remains of a deserted village, reputed by local folklore to have been a thriving community all those centuries ago on this windswept hill.

Access:
Although a public footpath passes close to the chapel, permission to visit it must be obtained from the adjacent farmhouse. Llanquian lies 1 mile east of Cowbridge along a track which branches off the A48 at Stalling Down.

Hen Eglwys, MARGAM

(SS 801 865)

Hen Eglwys ('old church') is a magnificently sited ruin, frowning impassively from a lofty hillside across the verdant expanse of Margam Park. The view to the west is less appealing, though: the glittering ribbon of the M4 cuts across the landscape, with the sprawling Margam and Port Talbot steelworks beyond. Travellers hurrying along the motorway may well have seen the ruined church silhouetted against the mountainous skyline, but its present visibility is due entirely to forest clearance in the region in the early 1950s. 'In a noble wood above the house stand the roofless walls of an ancient church with traces of a churchyard enclosure round it,' wrote the Revd William Thomas during a tour of Wales in 1787 (in a letter reprinted in *Archaeologia Cambrensis*). The house he referred to was that of Margam itself, seat of the powerful Mansels, which was built within the remains of a medieval abbey.

The Cistercian establishment at Margam was founded in 1147 and gradually acquired extensive properties in the surrounding countryside. Most of these outlying estates, or granges, had chapels for the use of the resident workers, and it may be that Hen Eglwys served this purpose as part of Cryke grange. However, there is little documentary evidence to confirm the existence of such a grange, and the chapel may instead have been used by the upland farmers working the leased-out abbey lands.

The fifteenth-century chapel of Hen Eglwys is a simple rectangular building, undivided into chancel and nave. A few surviving fragments of dressed stone indicate that the spacious gable windows were richly decorated in the Perpendicular style.

There is said to have been a holy well within the churchyard, dedicated (like the chapel) to St Mary, but a much more impressive well lies to the north in the Cwm Maelog dingle – a vaulted baptistry not marked on OS maps, nor easily spotted, for it lies on the hillside below the waymarked footpath. A spring of cold, clear water runs through the little building into a sunken bath in the floor. A third holy well, Ffynnon Bedr, is prominently marked on OS maps, 500 yd west of Margam village, but it is a disappointment: a few stone slabs covering a trickling spring.

Hen Eglwys, Margam: jagged openings mark the site of richly-decorated windows

Margam itself has other delights to offer the visitor. There is a deer park with its arboreal walks, a magnificent eighteenth-century orangery, a ruined thirteenth-century chapter house, and also the Margam Stones Museum, which boasts the finest collection of Dark Age and medieval stone monuments in Wales.

Access:
Freely accessible. Several waymarked footpaths lead up the steep hillside to the church. This overlooks Margam village which is 2½ miles south-east of Port Talbot, off the M4 at junction 38.

St Roque's Chapel, MERTHYR MAWR
(SS 889 781)

Relics from early Christian times abound at Merthyr Mawr. In the graveyard of the Victorian parish church there is a notable collection of carved and inscribed memorial stones dating from between the fifth and eleventh centuries, the only surviving evidence of a monastic centre reputedly founded here by St Teilo. And this area of the beautiful Vale of Glamorgan is also dominated by a legacy of medieval monuments – from the secular strength of Ogmore and Candleston castles, to the ecclesiastical glories of the Norman priory at Ewenni.

St Roque's chapel is a less well-known witness to the faith of the area's medieval inhabitants. Although it is one of the smallest chapels included in this guide (it measures only 17 ft × 22 ft), it is nevertheless one of the most intact, lacking only a roof and glazed windows. An elaborate bell-cote with finely dressed stonework has managed to survive precariously on the west gable.

St Roque's lies on wooded Chapel Hill overlooking the winding course of the Ogmore river. The existing building was probably built in the fifteenth century by the Stradlings of St Donats, lords of the surrounding estate. The grounds have been landscaped by the present incumbents of the adjacent Merthyr Mawr House, and in spring the little chapel is encircled by a mass of bluebells and daffodils; in summer

A 'four-centred' doorway leads into the tiny, late medieval oratory of St Roque's, Merthyr Mawr

the roses take over. The chapel is also set within the less obvious remains of an Iron Age hill-fort, and even more unexpected is the huge pothole which borders the enclosure. Part of the river follows a subterranean course through this 70-ft deep chasm.

The building contains two early Christian burial stones, which were brought here from elsewhere in the vicinity. The largest is a 7-ft high wheel-cross known as the 'Goblin Stone' – after its reputed guardian sprite, to which is attributed the antisocial habit of seizing passers-by and forcing their hands and feet through holes in the cross-head! The back and sides of the cross are enriched with key-work decorations, while on the front is a panel faintly inscribed with a Latin verse recording a property or land grant. The smaller stone is the base of a similar eleventh-century cross, with an unusually lengthy inscription which reads: 'Conbelan placed this cross for his soul [and the souls] of St Glywys, of Nerttan, and of his brother and his father. Prepared by me + Sciloc.'

It would be reasonable to assume that there was a chapel on this hill long before the existing structure was built. Many churches were built within prehistoric enclosures, possibly in an attempt to 'cleanse' a pagan area during the Dark and Middle Ages. A hint of the early origin of St Roque's chapel is provided by the seventh-century *Life of St Samson of Dol*, one-time abbot of Caldey Island monastery, Dyfed. According to the biography, St Samson left the island in a boat with some companions, and reached a 'desert' on the shores of the 'Severn sea'. They found a headland crowned by the remains of an ancient 'castle' and there set up a camp and a timber church. Samson, however, went off to live in solitude in a nearby cave, and created a spring of fresh water by driving his staff into the ground. Details of the story compare strikingly with the existing topography of the Merthyr Mawr district – a desert (the nearby sand dunes), hill-fort, church and cave can all be found here – and although the Stackpole area of South Pembrokeshire is often linked with this tale, the unknown author may well have had mysterious Chapel Hill in mind when chronicling the endeavours of this Dark Age saint.

Access:
The chapel is situated in the privately owned grounds of Merthyr

Mawr House, and permission to visit it must be obtained from the house. Merthyr Mawr village lies 1½ miles south-west of Bridgend, off the A48.

St Gwynno's Church, VAYNOR
(SO 048 103)

It is now a lot easier to reach the small upland village of Vaynor than it was 180 years ago, if we are to believe the historian Theophilus Jones:

> There is no village or even a single house adjoining the church; the roads in the approach to it are impassable by carriage and cannot without danger be travelled on horseback unless it be upon the small sure-footed ponies of the county.

Even today, the steep, twisting roads can be a frustrating obstacle course for the fast-lane motorist. Nevertheless, Vaynor was once a much frequented meeting place for the revivalist leaders of the eighteenth century, Howell Harris and John Wesley among them.

Vaynor lies on the north side of the river Taf, the ancient boundary formerly demarcating the old counties of Glamorgan and Brecon. The village is no more than a handful of scattered buildings (including a pub and an incongruous Italianate villa), a castle mound, and the parish church, clinging to the steep sides of the wooded limestone gorge. All that survives of the old church of St Gwynno is the crumbling tower; the rest of the building was demolished in 1868 and a new church built nearby. Jones provides us with an unwelcoming picture of the building as it appeared at the beginning of the nineteenth century:

> This building houses a small tower with two bells, and consists of a nave and chancel only; is low and dark, the roof not ceiled, the floor of earth and uneven, the seats decayed and irregular . . .

A photograph taken before demolition shows a plain and simple church, structurally undivided into a chancel and nave, with a south

Tottering tombstones and the crumbling tower at Vaynor old church

porch. Now only the tower rears above the narrow hillside graveyard, rank with undergrowth and tottering tombstones. The foundations of the rest of the building can just be traced among the weeds. The remains are difficult to date; archive sources suggest the main body of the church could have been thirteenth- or fourteenth-century, but the tower is much later, possibly sixteenth-century, and was built *within* the west end of the nave. The castellated parapet to the gabled roof is also an unusual feature, but a change in the stonework shows that it is a later addition.

There are many noteworthy headstone inscriptions for the dedicated enthusiast to hunt up in the tangled graveyard. Richard Crawshay's is the best known; a 10-ton slab of polished stone covers the resting place of this member of the Merthyr dynasty of ironmasters. It bears the curious inscription 'GOD FORGIVE ME'. A less portentous epitaph commemorates a reputedly rejected, broken-hearted suitor:

> Here lies the body of Gruffydd Shôn
> Covered here with earth and stone,
> You may sweep it up or leave it alone,
> It will be just the same to Gruffydd Shôn.

One more epitaph deserves to be singled out before we take our leave of Vaynor. A re-used plaque set into the west wall of the Victorian church commemorates Catherine Morgan, who died in 1794 at the ripe old age of 106:

> She was born in the third Year
> of the Reign of King James II
> And lived under seven Reigns.

A marvel of longevity noteworthy even today!

Access:
The old church lies in the graveyard beside the nineteenth-century parish church at Vaynor, just off the road to Pontscticill reservoir. From Merthyr Tydfil follow the A470 to Brecon for about 1 mile, and then turn right along the road to the reservoir. The turning right off this road, which takes you to the church, is after 2¼ miles.

St Mary's Church, CAERAU

(ST 135 751)

Having arrived at Cardiff on a day drizzling with rain, and in a crowded, noisy train, the solitude and peace offered by this church was gratefully anticipated. But what a disappointment – and what a warning to us!

Instead of an empty, echoing shell, or a ruin dignified by a wreath of ivy, the old parish church of Caerau is a crumbling, vandalized shell which has been subjected to so many indignities that the greatest shame is that it should be left standing for people to see. The walls are covered in graffiti and splashed with paint. The interior is choked with fallen rubble, domestic refuse and broken memorial stones. Some of the crumbling walls have been hastily propped up with concrete blocks. In a vain attempt to avoid further desecrations an ugly modern porch with a steel door has been erected around the remains of the original entrance.

The presence of a vast suburban housing estate at the foot of the hill has led to the church being singled out as a handy target for vandalism. This is a great pity, for the damage has been wrought only within the last decade, and the surrounding area has the potential of an important venue for those interested in our heritage. The church itself lies within the north-east corner of one of the largest prehistoric hill-forts in South Wales. The whole of the 12-acre hilltop is encircled by the multiple ramparts of an Iron Age stronghold, while behind the church is an impressive medieval ringwork, the original earth and timber castle of the Norman lords of Caerau.

But let us return to the sad church. This was formerly a subsidiary chapel of Llandaf Cathedral, and became a separate parish church at the Reformation in the mid-sixteenth century. The core of the existing building, as architectural details indicate, is thirteenth-century, with later-medieval additions including a vaulted porch and a tall tower with a gabled, or 'saddleback', roof. There is a roughly-built chapel on the north side of the nave, constructed probably after 1885, in which year the church was thoroughly restored. It was during this drastic restoration that several monuments of the wealthy Mathews family, one-time patrons of the church, were lost. In one corner of the nave a narrow

St Mary's, Caerau: a much-vandalized hilltop ruin

stone stairway leads to the first floor of the tower, but the upper chambers and belfry could only have been reached by ladders. Ruinous though the nave is, the chancel has fared worse, and most of it has been demolished. A cement screen now fills the chancel arch through which the medieval congregation would have looked towards the high altar.

Access:
The church itself is not open to the public, although a footpath crosses through the graveyard and hill-fort. Caerau is a suburb of Ely, 3 miles west of Cardiff along the A48. The road to the church starts from the rear of a sub-post office in Church Road.

St Mary's Church, CARDIFF

(ST 155 803)

Few people passing through this busy metropolis are aware of the 'lost church' of St Mary's. The imposing castle and the National Museum of Wales would seem to capture the attention of the majority of those who visit the city. However, the ruins of St Mary's church in Cardiff's suburbs have one distinct advantage over these two attractions: there is no entry fee! The remains themselves are not as impressive or as historically important as some of those included in this book, but what does remain has been tastefully laid out in a public park.

The church probably developed from a medieval chapel-of-ease mentioned in thirteenth-century documents, and the chancel may correspond to that building. From pictorial and written evidence of architectural details noted before demolition, it is clear that in the fifteenth or sixteenth centuries the existing nave and south porch were added, and the whole church was renovated in the nineteenth century. At the beginning of this century the redundant building was demolished, and in 1973 the few remains were landscaped by Cardiff County Council. The foundations have been exposed and the surrounding graveyard cleared of headstones and laid out as a garden, with pathways, shrubs and plants. Less thoughtful is the use to which the old headstones have been put. They lie unceremoniously on the floor as paving slabs, so that in time the names of those they commemorate will be lost to us.

Access:
The site of St Mary's is located at Whitchurch off Old Church Road, between the A4045 and A470; a gate in a walled garden opposite the Fox and Hounds Inn leads into the churchyard.

East Orchard, St Athan
(ST 029 681)

The countryside around East Orchard is grey and bleak, scarred by quarries and industrial buildings with the omnipresent silhouette of the Aberthaw power station dominating the skyline. Thankfully, trees hide most of this from the visitor to East Orchard, and in summer the whole of this remarkable complex of buildings is enveloped in shady foliage. Also hidden by the trees, and in an equal state of decay, is a sprawling group of buildings misleadingly named on the OS map as a 'castle'.

The chapel was not built to serve any village or settlement, but rather to cater for the spiritual needs of the well-to-do lords of the manor. In fact, East Orchard was an undefended dwelling of the Berkerolle family. Their great hall stands in skeletal ruin on the eastern edge of the hillside, with the outbuildings (including a retainers' hall, barn and dovecot) on higher ground to the west. The chapel stands parallel to the hall, and can be identified by its east-west orientation, large window openings (sadly robbed of their dressed stones), and a piscina in the south wall.

In 1411 the manor passed to the influential Stradlings of St Donat's, and then into the hands of the Jones family of Fonmon in the late eighteenth century. Thereafter the whole complex was abandoned and left to decay. The nearby parish church of St Athan contains two impressive effigies of members of the Berkerolle family, but the crumbling walls of East Orchard are a more eloquent memorial to the past glories of this Glamorganshire family.

Access:
The remains of the manor are on private land, but a public footpath crosses the site. This footpath can be followed east from St Athan village, or from the B4265 just west of where that road crosses the river Thaw.

St Fagan's Chapel, St FAGANS
(ST 119 773)

St Fagans is best known for its magnificent Elizabethan mansion and the Welsh Folk Museum, whose re-created buildings reflect the architecture and culture of rural Wales. But long before the great house was raised within the walls of a thirteenth-century castle there was a church here, built to serve the needs of a medieval village. In the last century more of the church survived above ground, including the west gable and what were then believed to have been the foundations of a tower, and the villagers recalled an excavation which took place here when a 'cartload of bones' was taken away. More intriguingly, one of the graves discovered was a 'stone coffin' containing a crude earthenware pot and a 'smooth sided stone', which sounds very much like a prehistoric burial.

More orthodox excavations in 1978–9 uncovered the remains of the building believed to have been the church. It had the usual east-west alignment, with an upper floor reached by a large stone stairway. A cruder post-Reformation building stood at right-angles to the church. Visitors today can see the buildings' (rather uninspiring!) foundations, which are set against a splendid backdrop of the castle and formal gardens.

Access:
Freely accessible, subject to admission to the Welsh Folk Museum.
St Fagans lies 4 miles east of Cardiff, off the A48 at Culverhouse Cross.

Upland Chapels

'Within Traen Baiden standeth a chapel called of that name, where service is said on Sundays and holy days.'

The site of the building that the antiquarian Rice Merrick saw and wrote about four hundred years ago is now no more than a vague hollow in a field beside a narrow, little-used lane. The adjacent mountainside is criss-crossed by deeply rutted tracks which date from medieval times, and is pock-marked with the hollowed foundations of dwelling house sites of the upland farmers who worshipped in the vanished chapel.

Capel Baiden is not the only lost church in the uplands of Glamorgan; similar mountain-top ruins can be discovered at Capel-y-fan (Mountain Ash), Forest chapel (Merthyr), Coly-uchaf and Capel Gwladys (Gelligaer) and Penrhys (Rhondda). None of the remains are very impressive and in some cases tradition alone indicates an ecclesiastical origin for sites which would otherwise be indistinguishable from

Conjectural reconstruction of the monastic chapel at Penrhys

humble peasant dwellings. Of these lesser sites we need only single out one for closer examination: the monastic chapel at Penrhys, above the Rhondda valley.

Penrhys today is a sprawling mountain-top council estate, a segregated urban settlement; five hundred years ago it was one of the most important places of pilgrimage in South Wales, and a large collection of medieval verse survives praising the virtues of the shrine of St Mary. The centre belonged to the Cistercian Abbey of Llantarnam in Gwent, and consisted of a group of at least three buildings: a chapel, hostelry and holy well. Today only the much-restored well survives intact, although a short length of the chapel wall remains above ground and has been incorporated into a modern boundary wall beside a bus-stop.

During the Reformation in the mid-sixteenth century, Henry VIII's iconoclastic vandals arrived at Penrhys one night and despoiled the chapel of its riches. The reputedly miracle-working image of the Virgin and child was taken away and burnt on a pyre. Bishop Latimer described the statue as 'the Devyll's instrument to brynge many (I feere) to eternal fyre', and is said to have flung a similar image out of the west window of St Paul's Cathedral in a zealous fit of rage. A modern statue of St Mary was set up in 1953 on the site of the chapel by the Roman Catholics of Penrhys, and it remains today, a lichen-spotted figure which gazes forlornly at the overshadowing estate.

Access:
The holy well at Penrhys is on the mountainside overlooking Llwynypia in the Rhondda Valley. A waymarked footpath leads to the well from the roundabout at the top of the B4542 Ystrad to Ferndale road.

West Aberthaw Chapel

(ST 024 667)

West Aberthaw chapel is almost indistinguishable from the farm buildings which surround it, and cattle are now tethered where the inhabitants of a now long-deserted village once worshipped. The whole complex – farm buildings, chapel and village earthworks – is over-shadowed by the towering stacks of the Aberthaw power station. It is not the most romantic of locations, but in the other direction you face the rolling countryside of the fertile Vale of Glamorgan. The chapel has only recently been re-discovered, although it was known to the eighteenth-century antiquarian Iolo Morgannwg, who also listed three other ruined chapels in the area (at Castleton, West Orchard and East Orchard; only the last survives above ground).

The building measures 21 ft in length and has an inserted upper floor; this cuts across a large window, now blocked, which formerly illumi-nated the altar. There is another blocked window in the south wall, above a small aumbry or piscina. These scant details proved sufficient for experts from the Royal Commission on Ancient and Historical Monuments to recognize this building as a former place of worship, and not a cattle-shed.

The chapel probably served the now deserted hamlet of West Aberthaw, of which all that remain today are two farms and a row of ploughed-down earthworks in the adjacent field.

Access:
The chapel stands in the farmyard of West Aberthaw farm, just off the B4265 to St Athan at Gilestan. At the side of the farmyard a public footpath leads south to the coast, and passes the chapel on the right.

THE
GOWER PENINSULA

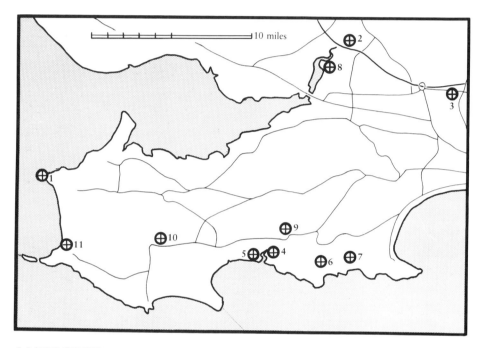

MAIN SITES

1. *St Cennydd's Hermitage, Burry Holms*
2. *St Teilo's Church, Llandeilo Tal-y-bont*
3. *St Cyfelach's Church, Llangyfelach*
4. *St Mary's Church, Pennard*
5. *Penmaen Old Church*

LESSER SITES

6. *Backinston Chapel*
7. *St Peter's Chapel, Caswell*
8. *St Michael's Chapel, Cwrt-y-carne*
9. *Trinity Well Chapel, Ilston*
10. *St Mary's Church, Knelston*
11. *Rhossili Old Church*

St Cennydd's Hermitage, BURRY HOLMS

(SS 401 926)

Beyond Rhossili at the western tip of Gower, the undulating limestone spine of the 'sea dragon' rears above the turbulent waters of the Bristol Channel. It appeared to the sea-roving Vikings, who named it 'Worm's Head', like a monstrous serpent. It was on this windswept promontory, according to legend, that the infant St Cennydd landed in a tiny wicker basket, having been set adrift in the Loughor estuary by his shameless parents in an attempt to conceal from the world the offspring of their adulterous union. Fed by the gulls which screech and wheel incessantly above the rock, the young saint grew up and lived on the narrow headland, until he was visited by an angel who told him to return to the mainland and establish a House of God. This he did, at Llangennith; but the island spell never left Cennydd, and he later retired

The pre-Norman timber church and enclosure at Burry Holms may have looked something like this

to nearby Burry Holms to live out the solitary life of a hermit.

This, according to local lore, is the origin of both Llangennith and Burry Holms churches, and there is no reason to doubt that a germ of truth lies embedded in the legends. Burry Holms is a low-lying island off the north-west tip of Gower. A visit there is akin to a pilgrimage, for not only is the nearest road over a mile distant, but you have to wait for low tide to cross to the island dry-shod. Nevertheless, the walk is well worth taking, and the intrepid visitor can approach the island either across the bird-haunted Llangennith Burrows, or along the firm, golden sands of Rhossili Bay, where the receding tide reveals the skeletons of wrecked ships.

There was a settlement here long before the first Christians set foot on the shores of Britain. Finds of simple chipped stone and flint tools indicate that Burry Holms was used as a temporary campsite and workplace by nomadic hunters during the Middle Stone Age, or Mesolithic period, some nine thousand years ago. Access to the spot was easier then, for the rising sea level following the retreat of the great Ice Age had yet to turn the Burry Holms plateau into an island. At some time during the Bronze Age (c. 2500–500 BC) a chieftain was buried under a cairn on the summit, and several centuries later a group of Iron Age settlers fortified their campsite by constructing a bank and ditch across the headland, from cliff-edge to cliff-edge. But the most striking relics of the island's long history are the remains of an ecclesiastical settlement which was established on the more sheltered east side from early times.

Nothing now survives of St Cennydd's Dark Age hermitage, nor of an oratory and cell founded here in the early twelfth century by the holy man Caradoc of Rhos (see p. 86) and mentioned in fourteenth-century manuscripts. During the succeeding centuries more substantial buildings replaced the simple pre-Norman structures, and it is these which now confront the visitor. The ruins of a small chapel and the extensive foundations of domestic buildings can be seen among the salt-scoured grass and weeds. Fragments remain too of a nearby post-Reformation cottage, built by some intrepid and hardy latter-day hermit.

However, the visible remains give little hint of the important discoveries made below ground during excavations carried out here between 1965 and 1968. It became clear to the archaeologists that the ruined stone buildings overlay dwelling sites which may date as far back as the Iron Age. It would appear that the east side of the island was first

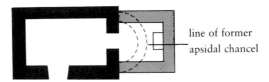

line of former
apsidal chancel

Plan of St Cennydd's hermitage, Burry Holms

used as a cemetery, which was enclosed by an oval, or boat-shaped, turf boundary wall. A small circular dwelling-hut of uncertain age stood nearby. Then a timber building (probably a chapel or oratory) was built within the enclosure, and another round hut erected just outside the boundary. This may have been the work of Caradoc, and the accompanying reconstruction drawing shows the early church as it may have appeared before the Norman invasion of Gower.

At some point in the twelfth century this simple wooden building was replaced by a slightly larger stone church, consisting of a nave with a semi-circular, or 'apsidal', chancel. Excavators also uncovered the remains of some contemporary (twelfth-century) dwellings beyond the south boundary wall of the graveyard, which in turn were overlaid by later domestic buildings. The complex reached its greatest extent in the fourteenth century, when a large hall, a schoolroom (*scriptorium*) and walled enclosures were added on the north and south sides of the church. The rounded chancel was also replaced by a larger and more typical square-ended one.

These excavations and resultant discoveries clearly highlight the problems facing anyone restricted to interpreting the history and archaeology of a site by a study of surface remains alone. The reasons for the decline of this remarkable group of buildings are not recorded, although the Reformation probably sounded the death-knell for pilgrimages to this remote island shrine, which would have meant an end to pilgrims' pious contributions to its upkeep.

Access:
The island can be reached on foot from either Llangennith village, or along the beach from Rhossili, but be sure to check out the tides in advance. Burry Holms lies at the north-western point of the Gower peninsula, beyond Llangennith Burrows.

St Teilo's Church,
LLANDEILO TAL-Y-BONT
(SN 585 030)

From its low-lying position on the tidal reaches of the river Loughor, the church of Llandeilo Tal-y-bont is commonly known as 'the church in the marsh', but the Welsh name is more informative, for it describes 'the church of St Teilo at the head of the bridge' – so named from its location at the first crossing-point of the river upstream of the old Roman fort of 'Leucarum' (Loughor). The importance of this crossing as an invasion route into West Wales was not lost on the Normans, who built two earthwork castles on opposite sides of the river. Only that on the south bank overlooking the church (and now positioned right next to the M4) appears in recorded history. This was the earth-and-timber stronghold of the Norman lord, Hugh de Meules, which was attacked and captured by the Welsh in 1215.

There may have been an early settlement grouped about the bridge-head church, but all that remains today is a decaying seventeenth-century farmstead. The role of the church itself was superseded in 1852 by a more accessible religious house at nearby Pontardulais, although annual services were held at the old site until 1973. Llandeilo was then de-consecrated, and for years suffered the indignities of vandalism and witchcraft rituals. By the early 1980s the church was rapidly falling into decay; the interior fittings had been removed, the slates stripped from the roof, and human remains dug up and strewn across the broken floor by vandals or black magicians.

Then, during a survey of the building, experts uncovered a remark-able series of medieval wall-paintings which had remained hidden for years beneath layers of whitewash. The importance of this otherwise nondescript building was then recognized, and it was decided to remove the paintings and disassemble the church for eventual re-erection at the Welsh Folk Museum, St Fagans.

In 1985 a team from the Department of Conservation at University College, Cardiff, skillfully removed the delicate paintings from the crumbling walls and took them to their laboratory, there to be consolidated and preserved before being replaced within the re-erected

An interior view of St Teilo's church, Llandeilo Tal-y-bont, taken during excavations before the building was disassembled

church. The earliest recognizable phase of decoration (probably early fifteenth-century) centred around a representation of St Katherine. It then seems that *c*. 1500 the interior was repainted with the figures of saints, and scenes from the passion of Christ.

Llandeilo Tal-y-bont has yet to be reborn in its new setting, and at the original site all that can be seen is the raised circular churchyard, with the unused masonry foundations and wall cores. However, the building itself exhibited many phases of work, from the twelfth to the eighteenth centuries, although the main part of the church was the simple rectangular chancel and nave of thirteenth–fourteenth-century date. At the beginning of the fifteenth century the church was extended on a fairly ambitious scale; a south aisle was added, foll-owed by a porch and north chapel. With the completion of the aisle and new entrance, the old west doorway into the nave was partially blocked and the upper half used as a window. More recent alterations included the rebuilding of the east chancel wall, and the insertion of Gothic-style windows. The remains of a stairway to the vanished rood-loft could be seen high up in the chancel wall, while below it on the south side of the arch was a 'squint', which enabled the congregation in the south aisle to catch a glimpse of the ceremonies taking place at the high altar.

Access:
At the time of writing the church has not yet been re-erected at St Fagans; at its original site remain the graveyard and a few ruined walls. From Pontardulais follow the B4296 towards Gorseinon to the village of Waungron. On the right a lane marked Castell Du Road leads to the church.

St Cyfelach's Church, LLANGYFELACH
(SS 646 990)

Only the much-restored tower survives of the old parish church at Llangyfelach; a violent storm in 1803 so severely wrecked the building that it had to be demolished, and a new church was built nearby. Imaginative locals (ever ready to dispense with a mundane explanation for any phenomenon) claim that the isolated tower is due entirely to the meddlings of the devil. The story goes that Satan tried to hamper re-building work on the church by stealing the materials every night; but when he tried to fly off with the newly-completed tower, the priest prayed aloud, made the sign of the cross and scared the devil into dropping the tower where it now stands.

The site itself is one of great antiquity. The unusually large, circular churchyard may well mark the boundary of the '*Monasterium*' reputedly founded here by St David in the sixth century. Some confirmation of the early origin of the church is provided by three Dark Age stones. One is a plain cross-stone of *c*. AD 600–800 set above the north door of the tower, and a few feet away stands the richly decorated base of a tenth-century cross. The modern church now contains the third stone, which is carved with a ring-cross and a latin inscription reading *CRUX·XPI* – 'The Cross of Christ'.

The surviving tower of the old parish church of Llangyfelach

Access:
*Freely accessible. The tower stands within the graveyard of
St Cyfelach's church, beside the B4489, 3½ miles north of Swansea.*

St Mary's Church, PENNARD, & PENMAEN

(SS 545 884 & 530 882)

Pennard and Penmaen beckon to each other across the expanse of Burry Pill, a muddy, meandering brook that flows from the limestone interior of Gower to the sea at Three Cliffs Bay. Both these 'lost' churches also have their lost villages and castles, relics from the twelfth-century Norman invasion of Gower. All were left to decay when a change in climatic conditions around the late Middle Ages rendered the area uninhabitable. The crumbling walls are now partly buried in the drifting sands which slowly swallowed up many low-lying coastal areas in the later Middle Ages: Margam, Merthyr Mawr and Rhossili were other victims in Glamorgan. The dunes are now grass-covered, undulating meadows pock-marked with scrubby hollows.

At Penmaen, one such hollow marks the site of the parish church. Look closely at the sides of the depression and you will see stonework behind the undergrowth. The outlines of a small and simple chancel and nave building can just be made out. There was even less to see before the site was excavated around 1860, and it was only the chance discovery of a fragment of painted glass on the surface of a dune which indicated the location of the church. When the remains were uncovered a number of hastily buried skeletons were found beneath the chancel floor, and the only access into the nave had been sealed off. This led the excavators to wonder if the bodies were those of plague victims. A less gruesome find was a small, intricately detailed bronze 'thurible' or incense burner, in the shape of the Holy City of Jerusalem. This can now be seen in the City Museum at Swansea.

Nothing remains above ground of the adjacent medieval village, although the earthworks of a Norman ringwork castle can be seen on the cliff edge. More surprising is the survival of a prehistoric burial chamber, which stands a dozen yards from the church, and which pre-dates the Norman settlement by at least four thousand years. What did the Christian inhabitants of the vanished settlement make of this megalithic relic of a pagan past?

Across the river stand the slightly more substantial remains of St Mary's church on Pennard Burrows. The ruined thirteenth-century castle is the more obvious monument here, but a short distance away (on what is now the golf course) a jagged stump of masonry marks the site of the old church. There is also a holy well dedicated to St Mary at the foot of the slope below the castle.

The creeping sand had begun to threaten the village as early as the fourteenth century, when a new church was built on 'safer' ground further inland. According to legend, however, the demise of Pennard was caused not by a natural phenomenon, but a supernatural one. The story goes that the proud and rapacious Norman lord of Pennard was feasting one night in the castle, when the sounds of ethereal music came floating over the dunes. Bewildered, he left the warmth of the great hall and crossed the sandy waste until he arrived at a strange gathering of elves and fairies dancing in the moonlight. Unable to comprehend what he saw, the headstrong Norman rushed among them, brandishing his sword and cursing them for disturbing his peace. The elves in turn cursed his foolishness and summoned up a great storm which buried the town and castle overnight in a sandy grave.

Access:
Both sites are freely accessible. Penmaen, which lies on the beautiful National Trust-owned headland, can be reached by a footpath from the post office beside the A4118, just west of Parkmill. Pennard can also be reached from Parkmill along a way marked footpath, or from Southgate by crossing the golf course.

Backinston Chapel

(SS 576 881)

Backinston is a tiny, forlorn ruin standing in the middle of a field above the winding Bishopston valley. The interior is a diminutive 17 ft x 10 ft and most of the walls still survive to their full height, though obscured by a huge ivy bush which has taken root in the crumbling stonework. Remarkable as one of the few survivors from among the many small chapels and oratories which existed during the Middle Ages in this region, this site may have been associated with the 'sanctuary' land held by the parish church in the area: any persecuted criminal could attempt to escape justice if he succeeded in reaching one of the recognized 'safe' chapels ahead of his pursuers. However, there is virtually no historical information about the site and it is unlikely that we will ever know for certain whether this was indeed a longed-for destination for fugitives all those years ago.

Backinston Chapel: a tiny ruin almost totally engulfed in ivy

This area of the Gower peninsula offers some splendid walks, particularly along the valley to the imposing parish church at Bishopston, which passes some of the natural wonders of this limestone landscape – 'dry' rivers, caves, chasms and subterranean streams.

Access:

Although the chapel itself is on private land, a public footpath crosses the edge of the field where it lies. Backinston can be found just off a waymarked path from Pyle to the Bishopston valley, about ¼ mile along.

St Peter's Chapel, CASWELL

(SS 590 883)

A visit to Caswell chapel is best in winter or spring before the rapacious undergrowth has a chance to engulf the ruins; by summer the site is carpeted in pungent wood garlic and shrouded in bushes.

This is one of Gower's most misunderstood sites, and explanations of its origins have ranged from a chantry chapel to an early Baptist chapel. The remains are clearly those of a medieval establishment, perhaps a subsidiary chapel of the parish church at nearby Bishopston, and comprise a group of three buildings: a priest's house, chapel and holy well. Apart from the tall east gable only the foundations remain of the chapel itself, and the nearby priest's cell has fared no better. When the site was excavated at the end of the last century, the east wall, with a window intact, survived, but this has now fallen.

A few feet beyond the cell, at the foot of a slope, is the holy well which bears a dedication to St Peter. First discovered during the nineteenth-century excavations, it was found to consist of a substantial masonry well-chamber; today, alas, only an alcove over a trickling spring remains.

Access:

The site can be reached from the hamlet of Oldway near Bishopston, just off the B4436. A footpath at the rear of Oldway housing estate leads down into the wooded Caswell valley, and the chapel lies in the bushes on the left. Alternatively, it is only a short walk up the valley from the beach at Caswell Bay.

St Michael's Chapel, CWRT-Y-CARNE
(SN 573 004)

Very little now remains of St Michael's chapel at Cwrt-y-carne: a grassy, rubble-filled hollow with a few upthrusting chunks of masonry, set in a marshy field beside the Loughor estuary. The building has been reduced to this state by a century of indifference and neglect, for as late as 1899 the chapel was substantially intact with walls surviving to roof height. It measured only 36 ft × 19 ft, and had a south porch (probably an addition) and a bell-cote over the west gable. In the twelfth century the lord of Llandeilo Tal-y-bont granted the lands at Cwrt-y-carne to Neath Abbey, and a grange was established here to control the property. The wording of the land-grant seems to imply that there was already a chapel here, but it would have been taken over and used by the lay-brothers working the abbey lands.

Access:
The scant remains of the chapel lie on private land opposite Cwrt-y-carne farm on the banks of the Loughor, 1 mile north-west of Gorseinon. A road leads down to the river from the village of Penyrheol.

Trinity Well Chapel, ILSTON
(SS 553 894)

Ilston chapel, like Caswell is another forgotten ruin mouldering away in a deep wooded valley. There is a pleasant signposted walk from

Parkmill which leads through the valley and passes within a few yards of the site, before emerging at the parish church of St Illtud at the head of the Ilston valley.

As the on-site information plaque informs us, the remains are those of a Baptist chapel built in 1649 – reputedly the first in Wales – which stood on, or near, the site of the medieval Trinity well chapel. The well still flows but the walls are in a poor state, despite efforts made in 1928 to preserve the ruins.

Access:
Freely accessible, and reached along a signposted footpath from the A4118 just east of Parkmill.

St Mary's Church, KNELSTON
(SS 468 890)

This site was originally known in Welsh as Llan y Tair Mair, 'the church of the three Marys', but the name later became corrupted to St Mary's, or St Maurice's. The three ladies referred to are the daughters of Anne, mother of the Virgin Mary. Local oral traditions abound which relate that Anne married three times, and by each husband bore a daughter who was given the name Mary.

The chapel has been mainly reduced to its stony foundations, although part of the east wall stands a few feet high. It is now impossible to say how old the building is, but it was in ruins by the late-seventeenth century. In 1697 the Gower antiquarian Issac Hamon wrote: 'there was in the time of King Charles I a pretty church but it hath been eversince open and uncovered and nothing done there but burialles.' There was also held to be a holy well nearby dedicated to St Mary, but the site of this has not been found.

Access:
Freely accessible. A signposted footpath to Burry leaves the A4118 just west of Knelston school, and passes through a farmyard. The

ruins lie on the right behind the farm buildings. A few yards further along the path is an impressive Bronze Age standing stone.

Rhossili Old Church

(SS 414 883)

This little village lies clustered about the medieval church at the end of the rocky peninsula, its historic features vying with the spectacular natural scenery for the attention of the visitor. The remains of an Iron Age hill-fort can be found on the nearby cliff top, and the numerous hang-gliders soaring above the bay have a better view than the land-bound visitor of the remarkable medieval 'strip fields' which survive east of the new church. Rhossili is one of the most popular places on the Gower with summer tourists, and so parking can be a problem in the high season.

The old church and village stood in the warren below the present settlement, but coastal erosion over the centuries has obliterated many of their features. Now the scant foundations of some houses can be seen on the left of the steep path down to the beach. A large sandy mound on the right is the site of the old church. It was briefly exposed by the Glamorgan–Gwent Archaeological Trust a few years ago, when the plan of the building was uncovered and photographs were taken of the simple painted wall decorations which had survived over the centuries, entombed by blown sand.

The small, austere parish church on the hill above the lost village contains an unexpected treasure which should not be missed: an elaborately decorated twelfth-century Norman doorway, which is likely to have formed the chancel arch of the old church in the warren.

Access:
Freely accessible. The remains lie below Rhossili village, off the B4247 at the end of the Gower Peninsula. A signposted footpath leads down the steep hillside to the beach, passing the site of the church on the right.

WEST WALES

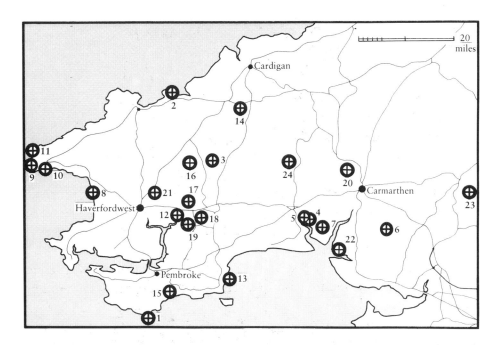

MAIN SITES

1. *St Govan's Chapel, Bosherston*
2. *St Brynach's Church, Dinas*
3. *St Teilo's Church, Llandeilo Llwydarth*
4. *St Teilo's Church, Llandeilo Abercywyn*
5. *St Michael's Church, Llanfihangel Abercywyn*
6. *Capel Dyddgen, Llangyndeyrn*
7. *Marbell Chapel, Llanybri*
8. *St Caradoc's Chapel, Newgale*
9. *St Justinian's Chapel*
10. *St Non's Chapel*
11. *St Patrick's Chapel*
12. *St John's Church, Slebech*
13. *Tenby Chantry Chapel*

LESSER SITES

14. *Pistyll Meugan, Eglwyswrw*
15. *Porth Clew Chapel, Freshwater East*
16. *St Brynach's Well, Henry's Moat*
17. *Llawhaden Chapel*
18. *Mounton Chapel, Narberth*
19. *Newton Old Church*
20. *Llanfihangel Croesfeini, Newchurch*
21. *St Leonard's Chapel, Rudbaxton*
22. *Hawton, St Ishmaels*
23. *Capel Dewi, Trapp*
24. *Capel Bettws, Trelech*

St Govan's Chapel, BOSHERSTON

(SR 967 929)

Perhaps nowhere else in Wales is the 'Age of the Saints' (a phrase coined by the scholar W.C. Borlase in reference to the Dark Ages in Wales) so eloquently evoked as at St Govan's. The spectacular, and to some eyes romantic, setting beside the wide seas and sheer cliffs of the Pembrokeshire coast attracts many visitors. Indeed this tiny chapel can even boast a royal visit, for in August 1902, Edward VII and his queen, Alexandra, stopped here on their way back from inspecting the Royal Yacht at Pembroke.

The lack of accurate historical information regarding St Govan is more than adequately compensated for by the wealth of folklore and legend. The identity of Govan has always been shrouded in mystery; one story tells us that he could possibly have been Gawain, the nephew of King Arthur, who was slain by Sir Launcelot and buried at this spot. A more suitable candidate, however, is Gobham, the Irish Abbot of

St Govan's chapel: an empty, echoing building hidden at the foot of the cliffs

Dairinis monastery, Wexford, who lived in the sixth century. He was said to have come ashore at this spot after being chased by pirates, and here he stayed for the rest of his life, teaching and preaching among the people of south Pembrokeshire. St Govan's feast day is celebrated on 26 March.

Whatever the traditions surrounding the chapel's origins during the Dark Ages, the existing structure is unlikely to have been built earlier than the thirteenth century, since no architectural features appear to indicate a pre-Norman date. The chapel lies wedged in a narrow coastal valley, looking as though it had hewn itself out of the surrounding rugged cliffs. A flight of steps – which, allegedly, can never be counted with the same result twice – leads down through the north doorway, into the dim interior of the small vaulted chamber. A door beside the altar leads to a narrow rock crevice, which legend tells opened to shelter the persecuted saint, whose rib marks can still be seen on the rock. A little spring beside the entrance is said never to flow over the chapel floor, and its healing waters used to be scooped up with a limpet shell. A second well, now dry, lies below the chapel and was widely used for curing rheumatism, lameness and failing eye-sight; some of those fortunate enough to receive a cure left behind their crutches on the altar as testimony to the healing properties of the water.

The chapel is in a good state of repair which, with a little help from the natural beauty of the spot, has ensured that its future is more promising than that of many similar chapels in less accessible places.

Access:
St Govan's chapel is accessible at all times of the year, except when the Castlemartin firing range is open. Details of firing times are available from local newspapers and the National Park authorities. The chapel lies south of Bosherston village, off the B4319 from Pembroke to Castlemartin, and there is ample parking on the cliff top.

St Brynach's Church, DINAS

(SN 014 400)

The church of St Brynach at Dinas Head must once have had one of the most spectacular views in West Wales, overlooking the coastal waters of St George's Channel from the low north Pembrokeshire cliffs. Sadly the little church paid for its privileged position, stone by stone, as the remorseless sea encroached on its foundations. In October 1859 the waves tore down the best part of the building, destroying in one tempestuous night the construction which had withstood centuries of wind and weather. On that same night many men lost their lives in the angry storms which lashed the whole Cardiganshire coast, taking a terrible toll of 113 ships and many houses built close to the shore. Another violent storm in 1979 further damaged the graveyard, and now only the west gable stands defiantly above a massive revetment wall holding back the crumbling cliff edge. Drawings of the church before the great storm illustrate a small, cruciform building with a double bell-cote over the gable. The surviving west doorway has a broad, four-centred arch, indicating a fifteenth-century date for the existing stonework. There is, however, no reason for doubting that a church stood on this site at an earlier date; coastal settings were favoured by early Christian missionaries, and this part of West Wales was heavily infiltrated by Irish settlers in the years following the collapse of Roman power during the late fourth and early fifth centuries. St Brynach was one such Dark Age immigrant who settled in this area, within sight of his homeland on the distant horizon.

The nearby craggy height of Carn Ingli, crowned with the tumbled walls of a Prehistoric hill-fort, was a favourite haunt of this saint, and it was believed that Brynach conversed with angels here: hence the peak's Medieval Latin name, 'Mons Angelorum'. Similarly, the magnificent 12 ft high Celtic cross at Nevern church, not far to the east, is linked with the Irish saint: he is said to have swapped it with St David for a loaf of bread! In fact, this richly decorated slab was painstakingly carved by a skilled mason around AD 1000 – long after those holy men were in their graves.

There are many other sites in this part of the country dedicated to St Brynach, but few equal in setting the ruined church at Dinas. At certain times during summer evensong is celebrated at the lost church; an evocative experience against the backdrop of the wild and beautiful Pembrokeshire coastline.

Access:
The rocky headland of Dinas forms part of the Pembrokeshire Coast National Park, and is situated between Cardigan and Fishguard off the A487. A signposted road to Cwm-yr-eglwys leads down to the coast, and the church lies in a hollow on the east side of the headland.

St Teilo's Church,
LLANDEILO LLWYDARTH
(SN 099 269)

The last seven decades have sadly reduced Llandeilo parish church from a decaying but intact building, into a weed covered ruin, lost among the labyrinthine country lanes of the Preseli Mountains. A declining rural community and a dwindling congregation appear to have signalled the death-knell for St Teilo's church.

This is one of the most ancient Christian sites in Wales, for although the surviving masonry is unlikely to be older than the thirteenth century, the discovery of several early Christian inscribed stones places the origin of Llandeilo as far back as *c.* AD 500. St Teilo was Bishop of Llandaf Cathedral in Glamorgan, who died in AD 566. There are many church sites in Wales dedicated to this early Celtic saint; indeed the original site of Llandeilo Llwydarth may well have been founded by Teilo himself. Two burial markers of fifth- or early sixth-century date formerly stood beside the entrance to the churchyard, but these have been moved to nearby Maenclochog parish church for safe-keeping. The Latin inscriptions engraved on the slabs commemorate Andagellus and Coimagnus, sons of Cavetus, and show that this site was used as a family mausoleum for local dignitaries. A third stone, removed from the neighbourhood to Cenarth in the Teifi valley, has an inscription to Andagellus' son, Curcagnus.

St Teilo's church was a small, plain building comprising only a chancel and nave. It was still roofed when the Royal Commission on Ancient and Historical Monuments carried out a survey here in the early 1920s, but now only the lower part of the walls survives, squatting in the middle of a tree-ringed graveyard. A short distance to the north-east lies the site of St Teilo's holy well, now encased in a brick pump-house which provides the adjacent farm with a plentiful supply of cold, clear water. In the not-too-distant past this well was renowned as a magical font with healing properties. The waters were believed to cure a variety of ills, including chest complaints, tuberculosis and whooping cough. Even in this century people were taking the waters, and during the First World War visitors dropped votive offerings of pins into the well, in the hope of ending hostilities. It was believed that the water would only be effective if drunk in the early morning out of 'penglog Teilo' – part of a human skull said to be that of St Teilo himself. This cup-shaped skull, burnished through constant use, was filled and handed to the pilgrim by the senior member of the Melchior family, the former owners of the adjacent farm and hereditary keepers of the skull. Sadly, this ancient and curious relic was purchased from the family by bogus museum officials in the 1950s and has never been seen again.

Access:
The remains of Llandeilo lie behind the farm of that name, between Llangolman and Maenclochog, off the B4313. From Maenclochog follow the lane signposted to Llangolman for about 1 mile. Where the road dips down into a wooded valley, a right-hand turn leads to the farm and church.

Llandeilo Abercywyn and Llanfihangel Abercywyn

(SN 303 134 & 309 130)

The twin churches of Llandeilo Abercywyn and Llanfihangel Abercywyn stand within sight of each other on the banks of the broad, winding estuary of the river Taff. The little Cywyn stream which separates these melancholy ruins also acts as a boundary between the two parishes, and its confluence ('aber') with the Taff has given this place its name. Despite their close proximity, the bird-filled marshes of the Cywyn valley prevent a direct route between the two churches, and so a long drive through twisting country lanes is needed to visit both. The effort is worth it, for Llandeilo and Llanfihangel are among the most atmospheric lost churches in Wales, not only for extent of their remains, but also for the beauty of their setting.

Llandeilo, St Teilo's church, is now a roofless building set in an open

Outlines of a blocked door can be seen beneath the west window at Llandeilo Abercywyn

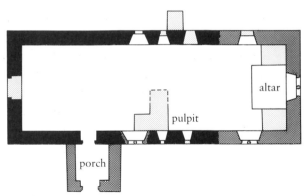

Plan of Llandeilo Abercywin

field beyond a 'modern' farm. In fact, one of the farm buildings is as old as the church itself – a hall-house with vaulted cellars, known as 'The Pilgrim's Rest' (of which more later). Beyond the last row of outbuildings a small ironwork gate gives access to the churchyard. Here stands the church, devoid of a roof and throttled by ivy, but otherwise in a fair state of preservation.

Llandeilo is a simple rectangular building of late thirteenth-century date, as the Early English pointed windows and doors indicate. The chancel was extended in the fifteenth century, and this work is distinguished by a different style of windows and, more obviously, by an abrupt change in the masonry from thin slabs to large, squared blocks of locally quarried mudstone. The south porch is an addition, and so too are the massive buttresses which prop up the gable wall of the chancel; evidently the low-lying, marshy nature of the ground caused headaches for those responsible for the upkeep of the building.

However, subsidence and structural decay was not the main cause for the gradual abandonment of Llandeilo: around the turn of this century its remote setting was cause enough, in an age of dwindling rural populations and more accessible places of worship nearer the larger villages and towns. When the Royal Commission on Ancient and Historical Monuments carried out a survey of the building during the First World War, it was still roofed, but in a dilapidated state. The succeeding years have greatly altered the picture.

Nearby St Michael's church at Llanfihangel was a ruin long before this century, but apart from the vanished north wall its shell remains complete to roof height – and photographs taken by the Royal Commission on Ancient and Historical Monuments before the First World War show a ruin which is little changed today. In 1848 a new church was built about 4 miles away in a more populated part of the parish, and the old St Michael's was left to decay. The replacement building is a curiously bland edifice lacking the charm and historical interest of its predecessor, although it does contain the original twelfth-century stone font from the old church.

At Llanfihangel the remains of the medieval settlement have been replaced by a large and rambling seventeenth-century farmhouse, but the eroded and overgrown earthworks of a motte and bailey castle can still be seen. The church stands on the opposite side of the farm to the castle, reflecting the balance between the twin spheres of medieval authority: the secular and the ecclesiastical. The existing building was probably constructed at the end of the twelfth century, and underwent little or no alteration until *c.* 1500 when a western tower was added.

The tower of Llanfihangel Abercywyn, a late-medieval addition to the original twelfth-century building

This acted as a porch to the nave, and the late-medieval outer doorway with an 'ogee' head provides a contrast with the pointed head of the earlier entrance. Another addition was the rood-loft over the chancel arch, which would have carried a wooden image of the crucifixion. Nothing survives of this today, the image no doubt having suffered the usual fate of many such Catholic 'idols' at the Reformation, but the crumbling stairway to the loft remains.

There is one very special feature of this site: Llanfihangel is commonly known as the 'Pilgrims' Church', and in the encircling graveyard can be seen six carved slabs said to mark the burial place of pilgrims who died here on their way to St David's Cathedral. An elaboration of this story tells how the weary pilgrims, on reaching this place, realized that they were nearing death. Each dug his own grave and lay down in it to die peacefully. The last of the ailing travellers placed the slabs over each of his companions' graves but, as he lay dying, had the strength to pull the slab only part of the way over his

A medieval effigy slab over the 'grave of the unknown pilgrim' at Llanfihangel Abercywyn (left) and the headstone of one of the medieval graves, showing a man on horseback (right)

own resting place. This tale was told to explain why one of the gravestones was crooked, but all appear to be neatly arranged today!

These carved slabs show male and female figures wearing stylized tunics and skirts, some holding weapons or a staff; another, smaller slab may commemorate a child's burial. All the graves have upright stones at the foot and head, some carved with the figure of a knight on horseback. The 'Pilgrims' Graves' were carved by a local craftsman in *c*. 1200, and some authorities believe they mark the final resting places of the Norman lords of Llanfihangel castle. But the pilgrim tradition cannot be so easily ignored, since when one of the graves was opened in 1838 half-a-dozen cockleshells were found beside the skeleton. This curious find may indicate that the pilgrim had made the long journey to Compostella in Spain, where shell badges were worn by visitors to the shrine of St James.

Access:
Both churches are freely accessible and can be reached from public footpaths. The easiest route is to follow the A40 west from Carmarthen, and turn left at the 'new' hilltop church of St Michaels. After 1¾ miles the road bends sharp left; carry straight on along the road to Trefenty farm, where a footpath leads through the farmyard and down to Llanfihangel. To Llandeilo, follow the road around the sharp bend, and continue for 2 miles to a crossroad on the hilltop. A signposted right-hand turn leads back downhill to the church.

Capel Dyddgen, LLANGYNDEYRN
(SN 465 126)

Only the ivy-shrouded tower now stands more than head-high at this forgotten, atmospheric site. A few scattered farms dot the surrounding landscape but there appears never to have been an adjoining village to provide the congregation for this thirteenth-century church.

The setting alone justifies a visit to this spot. Behind the old church the mountainside rises to a craggy ridge, honeycombed with caverns, while to the north and east stretches an uninterrupted view of the rolling Carmarthenshire countryside to the distant, hazy peaks of the Preseli Mountains.

Capel Dyddgen, or Llanlothegeyn as it was named in a fourteenth-century document, may have been built in this remote upland spot to serve the needs of a small community of woollen traders. By 1540 there were no fewer than seven woollen mills on the 1½ mile long Drysgeirch stream which gushes out from the rock just west of the church. There may, however, have been a more sinister reason behind the establishment of a Christian shrine here. On the bleak and rocky mountain top to the east is a surprising collection of prehistoric monuments – megalithic tombs, standing stones, burial chambers – and so Capel Dyddgen may have been built to symbolize the power of the Church over a 'pagan' area. Now the broken church and the tumbled megaliths can be viewed simply as representatives of the religious beliefs of long-departed peoples.

The decline and demise of Capel Dyddgen has gone unrecorded. By the beginning of the nineteenth century it was in ruins, as the Pembrokeshire antiquarian Richard Fenton indicated in his description of 'the ruins of a very neat chapel, the shell pretty entire, a neat tower with battlements, and a handsome archway leading to the chancel'. Fenton's 'neat' tower still stands, though it is partially ruined and completely wreathed in vegetation. It has a vaulted ground floor which served as an entrance porch, and an upper floor which could only have been reached by a ladder from the nave. A prominent straight joint in the masonry shows that the tower was added to the earlier chancel and nave, probably in the fourteenth or fifteenth century. There is a story that the original bell survived until a few years ago, when some youths stole it from the tower, only to lose it in the nearby rocks.

Access:
The church is on private land but is visible from an adjacent road. From either Carmarthen or Pontyberem follow the B4306 to the hillside village of Crwbin. Take the minor road to Felindre opposite the Three Compasses Inn and after ½ mile the church will be seen in a field on the right.

Marbell Chapel, LLANYBRI

(SN 337 126)

Llanybri is a village of surprises, set near the tip of a rolling, wedge-shaped headland between the Taf and Towy estuaries. The hill top settlement is approached by a maze of narrow, hedged lanes, all converging in the very heart of the village. Here we find the village green, and on it the skeletal hulk of what was once a church.

This is no shy ruin, decorously clothed in ivy, lying in wait to catch unawares the adventurous rambler stumbling through some unfrequented wood: the remains of 'Marbell' church stand upright and proud opposite the present-day post office and the Farmer's Arms public house.

A photograph taken around the time of the First World War, and published in the *Carmarthenshire Inventory of Ancient Monuments* (1917), shows the building as a typical early nineteenth-century Nonconformist chapel, with gleaming whitewashed walls and large, square-headed sash windows. Only the stunted tower hinted at a greater

The east end and stunted tower of the modified medieval chapel at Llanybri

antiquity to the outside observer. The upper part of the tower had been dismantled and the pyramidal roof added in the first half of the nineteenth century, when the building was damaged by fire. Another conflagration in more recent times reduced Marbell church to its present state. Now only the vaulted ground floor of the tower remains, with an inaccessible upper chamber, but it would originally have appeared similar to the fourteenth-century tower at the mother church of Llanstaffan, nearby: a tall, three or four storied structure rising from a massive splayed base to a battlemented parapet. The rest of the building comprised an unusually narrow and long nave and chancel which, in contrast to the usual structure of many Welsh churches, were not structurally divided by a cross-wall. There are two finely decorated Perpendicular windows in the end wall of the chancel, but the rest of the building between the altar-step and the tower appears to have been rebuilt – perhaps in the eighteenth century when this medieval chapel was sold to the Nonconformist Dissenters.

There is one other feature of this building that should not be missed. Above the entrance to the tower there is a mysterious stone slab set into the wall. The silent ruins will never divulge the answer to the question asked by visitor and local alike: what was the event in 1879 which so moved the villagers that they carved a clock face on to the stone, dated that year and with the clock hands perpetually frozen at five-to-ten?

Access:
Freely accessible. Llanybri village lies about 1½ miles north-west of Llansteffan, off the B4312. Other signposted roads can be followed from Carmarthen or the A40 to Haverfordwest.

St Caradoc's Chapel, NEWGALE
(SM 854 209)

Few authenticated facts about this Pembrokeshire hermit 'saint' survive, but this is more than adequately made up for by a wealth of legends. It is believed that Caradoc began his career as a royal kennel-keeper to the eleventh-century Welsh ruler of Dyfed, but this ended in dismal failure when he lost the dogs! Beating a hasty retreat from the king's wrath, Caradoc decided to try his luck with the Church and, after being ordained at Llandaf Cathedral in Glamorgan, he began to spread the good word far and wide. His second career choice was ultimately a triumph, and his fame as a holy man and miracle worker endured long after his death in 1124.

Many miracles have been attributed to the hermit Caradoc. He is said to have healed tumours simply by touch, and was able to turn fish into coins for the poor. Once, when Vikings attempted to kidnap him, he immobilized their longship. There is also the curious story, recounted by the twelfth-century cleric and historian Gerald of Wales, that when Caradoc's coffin was being carried across Newgale Sands for burial at St David's, a sudden, heavy rainstorm failed to wet the coffin and its silken covering. As further proof of his divinity, his body remained incorrupt for many years; and, when his contemporary the historian William of Malmesbury tried to make off with a finger as a relic, he had a dreadful fright when the blessed hermit jerked his hand away!

Gerald of Wales championed the cause of the hermit with Pope Innocent III, but despite all the reported miracles Caradoc was never officially accepted into the company of saints. Nevertheless, he now rests in good company at St David's Cathedral, and his splendid fourteenth-century tomb-effigy can be seen inside the Cathedral.

Caradoc was responsible for re-founding the shrine of St Cennydd at Llangennith, Gower, and also the nearby oratory on Burry Holms (see p. 59). On the bleakly beautiful coast at Newgale there stood another chapel dedicated to Caradoc, though whether it was founded by the hermit-saint himself, or built to commemorate the miraculous funeral procession, is not certain. At the beginning of the nineteenth century the decaying chapel was described by the antiquarian Richard Fenton as a 'long narrow building' constructed from the large smooth beach pebbles and mortar. In both its situation and plan it resembled St Patrick's chapel near St David's (see p. 91). Sadly, the frequent storms which sweep across the bay have long reduced the chapel to a faint hollow in the salt-scoured grass above the beach.

Access:
The site of St Caradoc's chapel lies on the coast at Newgale, on the south side of a small stream valley which opens on to the beach. The ruins of an old colliery can be seen near by, and at low tide the traces of ancient 'drowned' forests can be seen on the sands. Newgale lies between Solfa and Broad Haven, off the A487.

Chapels of the St David's peninsula

The rugged St David's peninsula – the Welsh Land's End – is dominated by the magnificent cathedral founded in the sixth century by Dewi Sant, the patron saint of Wales. The great veneration attached to Dewi's shrine during the Middle Ages is indicated by the assertion that two pilgrimages here were considered to be the equivalent of one to Rome. The site's significance is further attested by the former existence of at least ten chapels in the area, which received the prayers and coins of pilgrims embarking for Ireland and other coastal destinations. The amount received from these chapels was substantial; in 1490 the sum of £11 was collected from St Non's, St Justinian's and Capel y Gwrhyd. Writing some sixty years after the Dissolution of the Monasteries under Henry VIII, the local historian George Owen recalled how money was once brought by the dishful to the cathedral, there to be divided among the canons and priests, 'the quantity not allowing them leisure to tell it'. Sadly, today only two of the chapels survive above ground.

St Justinian's Chapel
(SM 724 253)

According to local lore, St Justinian was a Dark Age holy man, a strict disciplinarian, who was murdered on Ramsey Island by his irate followers and buried on the site of the existing chapel ruin. A less credible story has the obstinate saint walking across the sea with his head tucked under his arm, to search for a suitable resting place on the mainland. In any case the saint's remains were later dug up and taken to the cathedral where they now lie, alongside those of the patron saint, in a sealed casket behind the high altar.

Excavations in 1933 uncovered the remains of an early Christian graveyard beneath the floor of the chapel. They also revealed the foundations of a much smaller and simpler chapel below the floor of the present one. The existing building was built just under five hundred years ago by Bishop Vaughan, a few decades before the Reformation brought in the sweeping changes which rendered the chapel redundant.

Access:
On private land, but visible from the roadside, St Justinian's chapel lies on the right-hand side of the road from the cathedral to the lifeboat station at St Justinian's Point.

St Non's Chapel
(SM 751 243)

This small building, which tradition identifies as an ancient chapel dedicated to St Non, has one of the finest locations in Wales. As far as the eye can see the waters of St Bride's Bay stretch towards the horizon, fringed on the distant left by the Marloes peninsula and the bird watcher's paradise of Skomer and Skokholm islands. Only a stone's throw from the ruined chapel walls, the igneous cliffs plunge into a swirling cauldron which, like other rocky bays on this part of the Pembrokeshire coast, has been the graveyard of many luckless vessels.

It was here, during one of the frequent sea storms, that Non gave birth to her son, David, or Dewi as he is known to the people he watches over. One of the many boulders which lie strewn about the cliff top is said to bear the fingermarks of Non, imprinted in the living rock during the birth pangs.

The only tangible relic of the early Christian foundation here is a

A fine coastal setting for the ruined chapel of St Non's

large slab on which is carved a simple ring-cross. This dates from *c*. AD 600–800 and has been set up against one corner of the chapel. When exactly the existing building was constructed is a question that cannot be answered. It is unlikely to be as old as the stone, but almost certainly pre-dates the earliest surviving reference to a 'chapel of the Blessed Non' in a fourteenth-century document. There are no datable features remaining in the austere ruin, and the great, rugged stones are silent about their history. With the Dissolution of the Monasteries in 1536, Catholic shrines were desecrated and pilgrimages discouraged; St Non's was put to more mundane uses, and at one time served as a leek garden. The nearby holy well, which is said to have burst into life at the same time as David, survived longer, and the waters were much sought-after to cure a variety of illnesses, including rheumatism, headaches and eye complaints.

The historian George Owen, writing in Browne Willis's *Survey* during the closing years of Queen Elizabeth I's reign, describes the scene at the well in the following way:

There is a fine well beside the chapel covered with a stone roof and enclosed within a wall and benches to sit upon around the wall. Some old simple people go still to visit this saint at some particular times, especially on St Non's day, March 2nd, which they keep holy, and offer pins, pebbles etc. at this well.

Access:

Freely accessible. The remains of the chapel and well lie on the coast along a signposted track ½ mile south of the cathedral city of St David's. The modern Catholic chapel near by contains many carved stones from Whitewell, a vanished medieval chapel which stood further north.

St Patrick's Chapel
(SM 734 272)

Little remains to be seen today, but excavations in 1924 uncovered the foundations of this small chapel, preserved beneath the sand on the shore of Whitesands Bay.

The single-roomed building measured just under 35 ft long, and was entered by a doorway in the south wall. Skeletal remains of at least five people were found beneath the floor at the west end, while a more complete skeleton of a young man was uncovered in front of the altar, at the opposite end of the building. The chapel had obviously been erected over an existing burial place but the question is, was the altar-side burial the focus for the stone church, or a later burial in that most sacred part of the building? The fact that the altar partly overlaid the feet of the skeleton might suggest the former. Unlike St Justinian's, this chapel appears to have been a previously undeveloped cemetery site which gave rise to the building of the church. No dating evidence was found, and the sixth–tenth-century date for the chapel proposed by the excavators cannot be authenticated because of a lack of sufficient datable material. As there is no surviving pre-Elizabethan reference to the site, it can be assumed that the chapel had been abandoned long before the Reformation, owing no doubt to the incursion of the sands. In the mid-nineteenth century the remains of a larger building were said to lie near by, but all traces of it have been obliterated by coastal erosion, a process which still threatens St Patrick's today.

Access:
The site of St Patrick's chapel lies on the right-hand side of the car-park at Whitesands Bay, off the B4583, 1½ miles north-east of St David's.

St John's Church, SLEBECH
(SN 032 138)

Along a shady pathway between the River Cleddau and Slebech Hall, the battlemented tower of St John's church rises proudly through the trees. Not only is Slebech the largest ruined church in West Wales, it is also one of the most substantial and impressive in the whole of Wales. Although the church itself has been restored during the last decade and is in a fair state of preservation, much of the encircling churchyard is a veritable jungle, and at certain times of the year only the lofty tower and the tops of the walls can be seen peering above a leafy shroud. The ornamental trees and shrubs which have sneaked up on the church were planted here by the affluent owners of the adjacent hall, also now sadly past its days of glory. The comparative remoteness of the site was enough to signal the downfall of the church, and in *c.* 1840 it was dismantled by its former landowners, and a replacement church built a mile or so away on the main Haverfordwest to Carmarthen road. This imposing edifice contains some of the monuments removed from the gutted building, including a weathered fifteenth-century alabaster tomb-effigy of a 'knight in shining armour' and his lady.

The origins of Slebech old church are linked with the Knights Hospitallers of St John of Jerusalem. Like their contemporaries, the Knights Templars, this military brotherhood had been formed to guide and protect pilgrims on the long and hazardous journey to the Holy

The sixteenth-century tower and north transept seen through the chancel arch of
St John's church, Slebech

Land. Establishments under the control of these warrior-monks sprang up all over Europe, and wealthy patrons contributed gifts of land and church revenues to the upkeep of their chivalrous ideal. Slebech was their Welsh headquarters or 'Commandery', but at the Dissolution of the Monasteries in 1536 the Order was suppressed and all their lands were confiscated by the Crown. Like many other monastic properties, Slebech was purchased by rich landowners (in this case the Barlow family), and the Hospitallers' church became the new parish church, serving the needs not only of the few parishioners, but also of the secular lords of Slebech Hall. Even after the destruction of the building (some four centuries after escaping relatively unscathed from the widespread destruction at the time of the Reformation), the old church of St John found a new use as an ornamental garden feature, so preserving it at least from further damage.

In plan the building forms an elongated cross, with two transepts, a lengthy chancel and a nave. The tower acts as an imposing entrance

An interior view of the nave. The door on the left leads into the tower

porch to the church, and is tucked in between the nave and the corner of the north transept. But like many churches this plan was only achieved after much rebuilding and modification. Most of the existing masonry is the work of the Hospitallers, and it is likely that the rather small nave is the oldest part of the building, dating to the thirteenth or fourteenth century. This modest structure appears to have been sufficient for the warrior-monks' needs until the latter part of the fifteenth century when, in the more settled years of the Tudor dynasty, the church was wholly transformed on an elaborate scale by piecemeal additions. These changes can be detected by the differing styles of windows and door-heads, and by the greater attention to fine detail evident in the surviving stonework.

The first alteration seems to have been the reconstruction of the chancel (it is, in fact, larger than the nave, an uncommon arrangement in parish churches). In the south wall is a large recess in which the knight's tomb was laid, and this was once arched over with an elaborately decorated stone canopy. Alas, not a scrap of this remains today. At the end of the fifteenth century the three-storey tower was added, its vaulted ground floor acting as a pretentious new approach to the nave, which was entered through a large 'Tudor' doorway with a

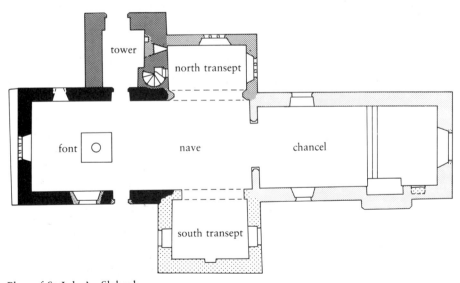

Plan of St John's, Slebech

carved head and heraldic shields around it. The upper part of the tower was probably rebuilt in the early sixteenth century, at which time the north transept was also constructed. Whether the balancing south transept was built at this time is uncertain, for it now displays only post-Reformation work using a liberal amount of brick and with much Classical detail. There is even a fireplace in one corner!

When the antiquarian Fenton visited Slebech at the beginning of the nineteenth century, he was one of the last travellers to describe the building as it appeared before it was dismantled:

> The floor of the nave is paved with small painted bricks . . . and that of the chancel with black and white marble. The roof . . . is ceiled with wood in square compartments, with a flower in each angle, and overlaid with the Barlow arms.

Not all the memorials were removed to the new church, and some tombstones lie hidden in the encroaching undergrowth. One slab, set up against the tower, is topped by a grinning Death's head, and bears the cautionary verse:

> Death does not spare
> Ye most deserved lives,
> Ye best of mothers & Ye best of wives.

This typically portentous eighteenth-century memorial was set up for Mary Mathias who died in 1730, aged eighty-two (a ripe old age for the time). Within the porch is a great chunk of a thousand-year-old yew, which originally had a width of almost 14 ft. A final, little-known feature deserves to be singled out: high up on the outside of the south wall of the chancel are two stones carved with the faint image of St John and the Lamb of God. Did they come from an earlier Hospitaller church on this site, to be built into the grandiose new chancel in the fifteenth century?

A further mystery surrounds this wooded site. Just east of the church on a low ridge jutting into the muddy tidal river, are two tree-covered mounds. Their age and function are unknown, and although often claimed to be Prehistoric burial mounds, the local name 'Holy Islands'

One of the headstones in the pets' cemetery

may imply an ecclesiastical connection. In the nineteenth century a late-medieval sword was found here, and the summit of the innermost mound has been used as a pets' cemetery: weathered headstones painstakingly carved with the names of those buried here rise up through the long grass and weeds.

Access:
Slebech church is freely accessible, and lies about 5 miles east of Haverfordwest. Follow the A40 towards Carmarthen to where a sign on the right points the way to Picton Castle Art Gallery. Follow this for about a mile, and take the first left-hand turn, which leads down a narrow road to Slebech House. A short walk from the road brings the visitor to the church. There is a longer walk to here from Blackpool Mill, just off the A40 at Canaston Bridge.

Tenby Chantry Chapel

(SN 134 004)

Tenby is a magnet for summer visitors to West Wales, but the wealth of historic features this coastal town has to offer can be sampled all year round. There is the medieval town wall with the celebrated 'five arches' gate; the crumbling castle nestling, Tintagel-like, on a promontory; and the noble parish church of St Mary, dominated by a 152 ft spire which forms a landmark for sailors miles out to sea. No visitor should miss the treasures kept in this church, such as the garish, life-sized figures of two seventeenth-century dignitaries, and the tomb-effigy of Mayor Thomas White who, in 1471, helped the future King Henry VII escape to Brittany during the Wars of the Roses.

It was during this period of the later Middle Ages that St Mary's church was extensively refurbished, and in the adjoining graveyard a two-storey building was constructed. This is believed to have been a chantry chapel, with a dwelling on the upper floor for the resident priests. All that now remains is a single wall, but the elaborate stone carvings make this little-known site quite outstanding. The wall is pierced by three openings: a window and two arched doorways with richly detailed jambs. The decorative head of another window has been built into the wall alongside the door. There is a strong tradition that this building formed part of a Carmelite friary established here in the fourteenth century, but this theory results from confusion between the Welsh names of Tenby and Denbigh in Clwyd, which had a genuine Carmelite House (see p. 136).

Access:
Freely accessible. The remains lie in the churchyard off Tudor Square in Tenby town centre. Not far away is the 'Tudor Merchant's House', a magnificent survivor of the medieval town, now in the care of the National Trust.

A re-used fragment of a richly decorated window can be seen (left) embedded in the remaining wall of Tenby chantry chapel (below)

Pistyll Meugan, EGLWYSWRW

(SN 172 379)

In years gone by the swiftly flowing spring at Pistyll Meugan farm near Eglwyswrw was a popular venue. Fairs, known as 'ffair Feugan', were held there on Ascension Day, on the Thursday after Trinity Sunday and the first Monday after St Martin's Day. The well is said to contain three distinct healing waters that never mix; one is considered good for the eyes, one for warts, and another for curing rheumatism, crippled joints and 'illnesses of the heart'. There also used to be a chapel near by, but during the Elizabethan period the very popularity of the well signalled its destruction. Three men, including the Pembrokeshire historian, George Owen, were instructed by the Privy Council to travel:

> to the place called St Meugans . . . and there to cause to be pulled down and utterlie destroyed all reliques and monumentes of that chapell not leaving one stone therof upon an other . . .

all in order to end such 'offrings and superstitious pilgrymages' taking place there. And in the event of any furtive rebuilding once the commissioners' backs were turned, it was proclaimed that any person who dared to 'repair either by night or daie the said chapell or well' was to be apprehended.

Though no stone survives to mark the site of the chapel today, the sacred spring still flows copiously, in defiance of the over-zealous Elizabethan reformers.

Access:
On private land. Pistyll Meugan farm lies beside the B4332 Boncath road, 2 miles east of Eglwyswrw, near Cardigan.

Porth Clew Chapel, FRESHWATER EAST

(SS 019 985)

This is an overgrown and undocumented ruin, standing forlorn in a meadow overlooking Freshwater East bay. Only the lancet windows and a little aumbrey hint at the ecclesiastical origin of the ivy-covered walls, which like St Non's and St Justinian's probably served the coastal travellers and sailors to this region. Earlier this century the remains of a doorway and a window could be traced in the north wall, and there were signs of the base of a stone altar beneath the east window.

Access:
On private land, but visible from the roadside. Freshwater East bay lies 3 miles south-east of Pembroke off the B4584 from Lamphey. At the village a minor road on the left beyond the Post Office leads back towards Lamphey; the chapel will be seen in a field just past the last house on the right.

St Brynach's Well, HENRY'S MOAT

(SN 054 280)

This little well-chapel has long been a ruin and only a few traces of it remain apart from the place-name and a gushing spring. From the account of Richard Fenton, the antiquarian rambler, it was in ruins by the beginning of the nineteenth century. He described the route to the spring thus: 'cross over a small brook to Brynach's Well, a redundant spring close to the ruins of an old chapel, having an upright rude stone pitched on end near it, marked with a cross'. This is presumably the Dark Age stone which now resides in the parish church at nearby Henry's Moat. The spring still flows strongly, but of its protective cover only a scattering of stones now remain. A hedge separates the well from the chapel site, which is a wilderness of undergrowth, obscuring the vague foundation of this lost shrine.

Access:
The remains lie on private land at Bernard's Well farm, in the foothills of the Preseli Mountains. The B4329 Haverfordwest to Cardigan road passes within a mile of the site, which is off a minor road signposted to Maenclochog.

Llawhaden Chapel
(SN 066 172)

The days of glory for this little village have long gone, and only the ruined splendour of the bishop's castle signifies to the visitor that Llawhaden was not always a sleepy hilltop village. In contrast to the austere lifestyles of the early Christian monks and hermits, the prelates of the medieval Church were not far removed from secular magnates, reaping the benefits of vast country estates, and indulging in sumptuous living quarters (the ruined palaces at nearby Lamphey and St David's give more than a hint of this). At Llawhaden the bishop's fortified residence was designed to withstand a fierce assault from anyone foolish enough to oppose the might and spiritual power of the Church.

Totally dwarfed by the glowering castle and overlooked by most visitors to Llawhaden is a tiny vaulted chapel, standing forlornly in a field beside the village. It is all that survives of a much larger hospital complex founded by Bishop Beck of St David's in 1287. At that time, the hospital offered shelter for the poor wayfarer in addition to caring for the sick and giving refuge to that dreaded outcast of medieval society, the leper. For this reason it was set beyond the confines of the original settlement, beside a road which led towards the town of Haverfordwest.

A chapel was a usual feature of such hospitals, and was often set at one end of the infirmary chamber so that bedridden patients might still be able to observe the religious ceremonies. Bishop Beck's chapel, which had an impressively lengthy dedication to St Mary the Virgin, St Thomas the Martyr and St Edmund the King, was no exception. The Llawhaden building is a simple oblong stone structure with a lofty vaulted roof, similar to St Govan's chapel (see p. 74), and it is now securely engulfed in ivy. With the sweeping changes brought about by the Reformation the hospital was closed and despoiled of its valuable goods. The sick and needy had to look elsewhere for comfort in the harsh Tudor society.

Access:
On private land, but visible from the roadside, the chapel at Llawhaden lies 6 miles east of Haverfordwest, off the A40. On approaching the village along the main road from Canaston Bridge, its remains lie at the rear of some houses on the left.

Mounton Chapel, NARBERTH
(SN 081 132)

This forlorn, little-known site lies some distance from the nearest road; standing alone in a field, its visitors are more often wild animals than people. The building is nevertheless surprisingly intact and has even retained its roof – although irremediable structural decay will soon bring about its end.

Mounton is a small and simple rectangular building, and was originally a single chamber. An inscription on a beam in the chancel commemorates the subdivision of the area into chancel and nave in 1743. The chapel's western doorway is covered by a small porch, and there is a single bell-cote on the gable above.

Records show that the chapel was in existence before the Reformation, and the few original details which survived the eighteenth-century restoration indicate that it was built probably in the thirteenth or fourteenth century. Mounton served the upland population of the large parish of Narberth; a declining rural population during the early years of this century signalled its decline and eventual abandonment.

Access:

On private land, although a public footpath passes the field in which the chapel stands. There are several paths to the site from the A4075 at Canaston Woods; all of the routes entail a long walk and an OS map is really needed here for the visitor to pick the most convenient route. A more clearly marked path can be followed north-west from Molleston Cross on a minor road which branches off the A478 at Narberth Bridge below the town.

Newton Old Church
(SN 066 133)

For nearly a century the old parish church of Newton, near Narberth, has been derelict, and the inevitable encroachment of undergrowth has turned the whole site into a veritable jungle. Lying in a dell, the ruined tower reaches out of a green sea of dense foliage like the hand of a drowning man. On one side of the forgotten graveyard is the parish holy well, an overgrown, marshy spring bursting out from under an overhanging rock. Local tradition does not recount whether it has been credited with any of the curative powers so often associated with such sources.

The interior of the church is so overgrown that in places exploration is only possible along narrow breaks between the crumbling walls and ranks of ferocious brambles and nettles. A curtain of overhanging ivy is parted to reveal a dark stairway leading up to the long-vanished rood loft, and the lancet windows are now filled with green leaves instead of stained glass. Despite this picture of decay the walls of the church are, at present, remarkably intact; even the vaulted tower retains its crumbling spiral stair, leading up to a dizzying vantage point from the topmost turret. The death-blow for this thirteenth-century church came with the merger of Newton with the adjoining parish of Slebech following which the church, remote from any town or village, was left to decay.

Access:

The church is on private land, although an unmarked public footpath crosses the adjoining field. Newton lies on the west side of the A4075 Canaston Bridge to Carew road, about 1½ miles from Canaston Bridge itself. Where the road emerges from Canaston Woods there is a sharp left-hand bend, and directly opposite it is the start of the path to the church.

Llanfihangel Croesfeini, NEWCHURCH
(SN 395 238)

The name of this little-known Dark Age and medieval site means 'the church of St Michael of the cross stones', and although nothing now survives above ground of the church, the two inscribed stones to which the name refers can be seen at the Carmarthen Museum, Abergwili. Both stones were set up around fifteen hundred years ago in memory of Dark Age dignitaries, namely Severinus and Cunegnus. In the Middle Ages the Normans established a large ringwork castle beside the Dark Age burial ground, and the chapel was presumably built (or rebuilt) at the same time. Some earthworks, possibly of a settlement, remain between the castle mound and chapel site. How long this site was occupied is not known, but at some time after the Reformation the chapel became redundant and was eventually demolished, the stones being used to build a nearby barn. The inscribed slabs nearly met with a similar fate before they were removed for safe-keeping. On the summit of the mountain which overlooks the site are the burial mounds of those who lived and died in this area nearly two thousand years before the arrival of Christianity, and it would seem that the memorials of their pagan culture have fared rather better.

Access:
On private land 3½ miles north-west of Carmarthen, beside a minor road from Ffynnon-ddrain to Newchurch. The site of the chapel and castle lie in a field on the right-hand side of the road, just before the small hamlet of Crug.

St Leonard's Chapel, RUDBAXTON

(SM 985 188)

This chapel was built just outside the massive ramparts of an Iron Age hill-fort, perhaps in order to sanctify this 'pagan' area. There are local legends of the 'Wild Hunt' with ghostly hounds seeking out lost souls. A more mundane explanation is that the chapel was built to serve the needs of a short-lived Norman settlement, since the fort was adapted as a ringwork and bailey castle in the twelfth century. In a medieval document the site is named as 'Capella Sci Leonardi de Castro Symonis', which means 'the chapel of St Leonard beside Simon's castle'. The fate of the castle itself is unrecorded, but the little chapel was still being used in the fourteenth century when, in 1398, the rector of nearby Rudbaxton was granted permission to celebrate mass here.

In common with many other ancient chapels, there is a holy well close by which is dedicated to the saint: it's stone cover bears the inscription 'Fons Leonardis'. The cold, clear waters were believed to be an effective cure for sore eyes. Sadly, the chapel is now lost to modern viewers, and only a slight earthwork marks it site.

Access:
On private land 3 miles north-east of Haverfordwest. The tree-covered earthworks of the hill-fort can be seen from the side of a minor road from Crundale to Clarbeston road.

Hawton, ST ISHMAELS

(SN 36? 07?: *exact location uncertain*)

Only when the muddy waters of the Tywi estuary recede at low tide will the dedicated visitor see the putative site of Hawton church and its lost village. A few scattered boulders and a seaweed-encrusted reef is said to mark the position of this latter-day Lyonesse or Atlantis.

It would appear that a church and settlement were established here in the thirteenth century, on what at that time was a low-lying coastal plain bordering the estuary. Sand-covered foundations have been recorded along the beach near St Ishmaels Point, and numerous finds of potsherds dating from the fourteenth to the sixteenth century point to the general location of this village. Some medieval and later documents refer to 'Halkyng' or 'Akenchurch', which were formerly thought to be other names for Hawton, but are now identified as referring to nearby Llansaint.

The Elizabethan cartographer Saxton marked Hawton church on the map of Carmarthenshire he made in 1576. So too did Speed in 1610, although by that time the village may have been little more than a memory: in 1606 a violent storm swept across the Bristol Channel, and the sea, 'having the appearance of mountains of fire', overwhelmed the little village. Reports of such a cataclysmic event need not be taken too literally, for it may have been a succession of storms, coupled with coastal erosion, which forced the gradual abandonment of the village and church and consigned them to the realm of legend.

Access:
The site of Hawton lies on the coast below the (surviving) medieval church of St Ishmael, on a minor but signposted road from Kidwelly to Ferryside.

Capel Dewi, TRAPP

(SN 659 178)

Capel Dewi – St David's chapel – occupies a spectacular location in the heart of the Dyfed Black Mountain, and just within the boundary of the Brecon Beacons National Park. From this hilltop site the whole of the verdant Cennen valley spreads before the visitor, with the distant peaks of the Preseli Mountains crowning the horizon. Across the valley stands the ruin of Carreg Cennen castle, perched on a sheer cliff like an eagle surveying the land for its prey. This magnificent Aruthurian ruin provides a dramatic contrast with the scant remains of Capel Dewi, a building of uncertain age and origin.

Sadly, only the low earthworks outlining the position of the chancel and nave are left of this holy site. An irregular mound of stones on one side could be the remains of a porch, or tower. A short distance away to the east is another oblong earthwork, perhaps all that has survived of the humble dwelling once occupied by an attendant priest.

Access:
This site is in a field beside a public footpath leading from Llwyndewi Craft Centre to Cwrt Bryn y Beirdd, a medieval mansion. Capel Dewi lies on the mountainside between the villages of Trapp and Drefach, 2½ miles east of the A483 Llandeilo to Ammanford road. The way to Trapp and Carreg Cennen castle is clearly signposted. There are many fine walks in this area, including a waymarked footpath along the Cennen valley, which passes Capel Dewi and the underground source of the river Loughor.

Capel Bettws, TRELECH
(SN 278 284)

Capel Bettws stands alone, remote from the more populated areas of old Carmarthenshire, and about 2 miles from the mother church at Trelech. The ruins are now very overgrown, set in a mossy mound and securely fenced in on all sides. Only the crumbling chancel arch, peeping over the bracken, gives any indication that here lies a building of note. In the surrounding fields are fragments of stonework and walling that once belonged to this imprisoned chapel. The remains consists of a chancel, nave and north aisle, of thirteenth- or fourteenth-century date. There is also a curious passage which leads from the aisle to the chancel, which was probably a 'passage-squint', enabling worshippers in the aisle to witness the rites taking place at the high altar. In 1710 chapel services were discontinued at this remote spot, resulting in the building's decline.

Access:
On private land south of Gilfachbetws farm, Capel Bettws lies 1 mile west of the B4229 St Clears to Meidrim road, about 4 miles north of Meidrim.

MID WALES AND THE MARCHES

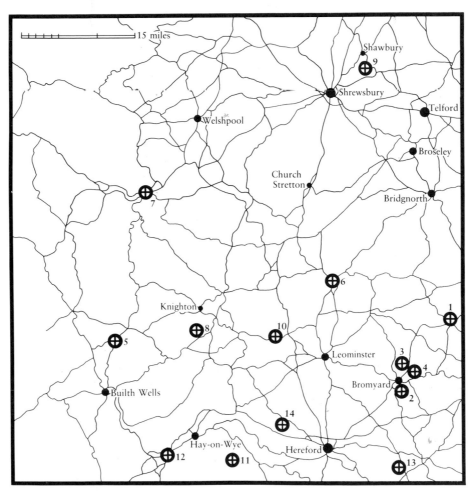

MAIN SITES

1. *St Michael's Church, Abberley*
2. *St Mary's Church, Avenbury*
3. *St Mary's Church, Edvin Loach*
4. *Lower Brockhampton Chapel*
5. *Capel Maelog, Llandrindod Wells*
6. *St Thomas' Chapel, Ludlow*
7. *St Mary's Church, Newton*
8. *Ednol Chapel, Old Radnor*
9. *Poynton Chapel*

10. *Shobdon Arches*
11. *Urishay Chapel, Peterchurch*

LESSER SITES

12. *Aberllynfi Chapel*
13. *All Saints Church, Brockhampton-by-Ross*
14. *St John's Church, Yazor*

St Michael's Church, ABBERLEY

(SO 753 680)

In a corner of Worcestershire, on the edge of the beautiful and lush valley of the river Teme, the Saxon chief Eobald chose to establish a settlement. He named his village 'Eoboldelega', which later became 'Abberley'. From these early beginnings Abberley became a village of some importance. In the seventh century St Augustine chose this site to meet the Welsh bishops, in a vain attempt to arrange a uniform celebration of Easter. The spot where they met lies near the main entrance of Abberley Hall School, and is known as 'Apostle's Oak'.

During the reign of Offa, King of Mercia, in the ninth century, a church and priest's house were built here, although their exact location was never recorded. After the Norman conquest the Manor of Abberley was given to Roger du Todeni, one of the Conqueror's most powerful barons. It was most probably he who built the church of St Michael on the foundations of the earlier church. This supposition was backed up by the discovery of a Saxon tomb cover, which had been used by the twelfth-century builders as a lintel.

From what remains today it is evident that St Michael's church must have been a magnificent Norman building. Despite alterations during the following centuries, its Norman character was retained before the church finally fell into decay in the middle of the nineteenth century. The chancel was restored between 1962 and 1964 and is now used for baptisms and the occasional evening service. A Gothic Victorian 'new' church was built adjacent to St Michael's in 1852.

The old St Michael's remains today as ruined walls, with a round-headed Norman arch leading into the nave. This appears to have been tastefully designed as a sitting area, with rose bushes climbing the crumbly, pale brown sandstone.

There are many interesting details to be seen inside the restored chancel, including Blamyre's Bell. This bell survived the Reformation and was brought here by John Blamyre, a Cumbrian abbot, whose blameless life inspired even the tyrannical Henry VIII to allow him to continue with his ecclesiastical vocation by making him rector of St Michael's.

During excavations carried out at Abberley in the 1960s, five fourteenth-century silver spoons were discovered sealed up in the walls. This surprising discovery is hard to explain, but it may be that these prized relics were hidden at the time of the Reformation and never recovered in less unsettled times. The original spoons were taken to the British Museum, although replicas can be seen in the museum at nearby Hartlebury Castle.

Access:
Abberley lies off the B4202 road to Clows Top, about 10 miles north-west of Worcester. The ruins are in the care of English Heritage and are well signposted from the village.

St Mary's Church, AVENBURY
(SO 662 532)

A dark and dreary churchyard ringed with a crumbling drystone wall encloses the remains of the old parish church of Avenbury. From the encircling cloak of vegetation rises the monolithic red sandstone mass of the tower, crowned with the skeletal remains of a timber roof. The interior is a precarious lattice of decaying floor beams, making exploration of this part of the building unadvisable.

When the Royal Commission on Ancient and Historical Monuments carried out a survey of St Mary's church in *c.* 1930 the building was in decay, but substantially intact. The succeeding years of neglect have taken their toll, and now only the tower and part of the chancel stand above the rubble-strewn graveyard; there are two surviving early Norman round-headed windows in the chancel wall. The Commission's survey indicated that Avenbury was a particularly complex building, formerly of greater extent: there was a thirteenth-century north aisle which had been blocked up at some uncertain date, and also a half-timbered south porch; none of these features can now be seen.

This gaunt ruin set in a gloomy, atmospheric valley has, unfortunately, found itself an occasional and less welcome congregation. At the time of our visit soon after midsummer eve, we found beneath the shelter of a large, twisted tree the remains of a hearth, a scatter of black feathers, and inverted timber crosses daubed with arcane symbols – all relics of an unchristian ceremony carried out at this deconsecrated ruin.

Access:
Avenbury lies in the valley bottom alongside the river Frome, about 1½ miles south-east of Bromyard. The easiest route is to follow the A44 to the outskirts of the town, and take the first turning on the right. At the crossroads take the right-hand turn and cross over a small bridge. A small lay-by marks the start of a short path to Avenbury.

St Mary's Church, EDVIN LOACH
(SO 663 585)

On a late summer's evening the setting sun floods the Herefordshire landscape with a mellow light, painting the weathered, pock-marked masonry of the Edvin Loach old church with a rich, golden glow. On a misty spring morning, or in the rich colours of autumn, this evocative ruin is imbued with a spirit of antiquity. Whatever the time of year, and regardless of the weather, the presence of this building is awe-inspiring. Set in a most pleasing and tranquil environment, this 'lost' church not only fulfils the Romantic ideal of the ruin but also retains the air of a House of God. It is not a particularly noticeable site; a few signposts point the way only to 'Edvin Loach', and it is the hilltop spire of the nineteenth-century church of St Mary which first catches the eye. There is ample parking in front of the churchyard gates, and just within, sheltered by a clump of ancient yews, is the rugged shell of the old church.

Look closely at the walls, for the stones have a tale to tell. The slabs of locally quarried mudstone have been arranged in a rare herringbone pattern, indicating that the core of the building is very early Norman

Saxon 'herringbone' masonry at St Mary's church, Edvin Loach

work or, more likely, late Saxon. The round-headed south doorway, with its plain and massive tympanum, is a typically ponderous Norman feature. So too are the few remaining windows – tiny unglazed slits in the walls. The utmost simplicity of this early church is further heightened by the liberal use of 'tufa' – a natural pumice-like stone formed in much the same way as stalactites, by a gradual accumulation of calcite particles. In places the walls look as if they have been constructed from chunks of bath sponge or Swiss cheese! At one end of St Mary's is a diminutive open-backed tower of sixteenth-century date, now held in one piece by metal bars. One of the windows still retains its original wooden frame.

The unusual name of the parish is said to derive from the Edeven or Edifen family who owned the surrounding land before it was divided into two centres, Edvin Loach and Edvin Ralph. A somewhat improbable story concerns two young men from the neighbouring parishes who were in love with the same girl. Their rivalry escalated into a feud, which ended in tragedy when a duel was arranged. The girl tried to intervene in the fight, but was inadvertently skewered on both their swords. The unfortunate lass is said to have been buried at the nearby church of Edvin Ralph which, incidentally, contains a very fine collection of medieval stone effigies.

Surprisingly for such a small building, Edvin Loach church remained in use until the late nineteenth century with little change to the fabric. The cramped and decaying building was obviously felt to be inadequate for the spiritual needs of the Victorian parishioners, and a new church was built alongside by the renowned church architect Sir George Gilbert Scott. This imposing edifice now contains some fittings removed from the Saxon church, including part of a Norman font and a fourteenth-century bell. For a time the two buildings remained in use together, as a photograph displayed on the wall of the new church shows; but decay soon set in, and the ruinous eleventh-century building was saved from further deterioration only when English Heritage undertook its consolidation and repair a few years ago.

Just beyond the crest of the hill stands Hope Farm, a half-timbered building of sixteenth-century origin. It may well have replaced an older manor which stood in the field behind the church. The site of this can be seen as a low circular mound ringed with a silted-up ditch: almost certainly the eroded remains of an earth and timber motte castle. Surprisingly this was missed by the Royal Commission on Ancient and Historical Monuments and Sir Nikolaus Pevsner, but did not escape the eye of the Worcestershire antiquarian Thomas Habington (1560–1647) who visited this hallowed place four centuries ago.

Access:
This atmospheric ruin is in the care of English Heritage and is freely accessible. From Bromyard follow the B4203 Upper Sapey road for 2 miles. Just before the hamlet of Sandy Cross a signposted left turn leads to Edvin Loach. Follow this road for a further 1¼ miles to where another left-hand turn leads to the church. Edvin Ralph lies north of Bromyard off the B4214.

Lower Brockhampton Chapel

(SO 687 560)

Lower Brockhampton Hall has aptly been described as the most photographed of National Trust properties, and who can fail to be charmed by the first glimpse of this black and white half-timbered house, mirrored in the still waters of an encircling moat? But unobtrusively situated at the back of the Hall is the old chapel, a ruined, roofless shell keeping company with mundane farm buildings. This little chapel was the private place of worship for the well-to-do lords of the manor, and was built in the late twelfth century. The manor itself was probably founded early in that century by the Brockhampton family, and passed through a variety of owners until it fell into neglect in the latter part of the eighteenth century. Both the hall and chapel bear witness to changing fashions over the years with the variety of architectural styles which have survived. The earliest part of the timber-framed Hall dates from *c.* 1390, but long before this the stone walls of the chapel were echoing to the prayers of worshippers. The round-headed inner arch of the doorway proclaims a Norman origin for the building, but the Early English and Perpendicular windows show that additions were carried out by later owners in the thirteenth, fourteenth and fifteenth centuries.

Many of the stones used in the walls are shaped blocks of tufa, a calcerous deposit which was quarried locally and also used extensively at nearby Avenbury and Edvin Loach churches (see pp. 111 and 112). Throughout the centuries the little chapel retained its original simple rectangular plan, the only alterations confined to finer details, such as new doors and windows in the fashionable styles of the Middle Ages. The adjacent Hall, however, was greatly modified in the more sophisticated and comfort-conscious post-Reformation period. Brick fireplaces with tall chimneys replaced the original open hearths, and further service ranges were added along one side of the Hall.

In the 1760s Brockhampton Court was built near by as the new seat of the local landowners. A few decades later a replacement church was built close to the Court, and the medieval chapel was left to decay.

Access:
Freely accessible. Brockhampton Hall is in the care of the National Trust, and is open from March to September and on Bank Holidays. It is situated in a valley bottom 2 miles east of Bromyard, and the access road is signposted from the A44.

Capel Maelog, LLANDRINDOD WELLS
(SO 067 615)

The mid-Wales spa town of Llandrindod Wells has recently been given a new lease of life with the inspired development of an annual 'Victorian week' in early September. Local people don frock-coats and crinolined dresses, and take part in a festival which highlights the town's nineteenth-century heritage. A lesser-known survivor of old Llandrindod is Capel Maelog, a 'lost' chapel which has been lost more than once in its long history. It is not known for certain when the building was abandoned (possibly in the late fifteenth century) but it decayed to such an extent that by the nineteenth century only local tradition could identify the field where it had once stood. In the mid-1980s this pleasant meadow succumbed to modern development when a housing estate was built on it. The Clwyd–Powys Archaeological Trust carried out a 'rescue' excavation and uncovered the foundations of a remarkable building preserved beneath the turf. After three seasons of painstaking archaeological work, the proposed development went ahead, obliterating the site of St Maelog's chapel.

But this was not the end of the story. Stones recovered from the dig were used to build an outline plan of the chapel elsewhere in Llandrindod, so that something of this ancient shrine is preserved for posterity. The excavations revealed that there was a Christian burial ground here long before the chapel was built; many graves, with their resident skeletons, were found beneath the floor of the building and in the encircling graveyard, which was enclosed by a low bank and a slight outer ditch. The first stone church was a typical chancel and nave structure, which was later modified into a unique lozenge-shaped plan

A reconstruction of Capel Maelog as it may have appeared in its final form, with two apsidal ends

by the addition of two half-round projections at either end of the building (see reconstruction drawing, above). Many of the stones were squared blocks of Roman masonry, probably robbed from the site of the abandoned fort at Castell Collen, about a mile to the west. No evidence was found to help date the earlier phases of Capel Maelog, but archaeologists believe that it was built during the twelfth century.

Although the stones of the chapel have been saved, less is known about the fate of a monolith which stood nearby, and which is said to have ambled down to a nearby stream for a drink at cock-crow! Such unlikely tales about animate rocks are widespread, and may reflect a distorted belief in the ancient mystical powers of sacred stones and running water.

Access:
The rebuilt foundations of Capel Maelog can be seen on the edge of the boating lake in Llandrindod Park, just south-east of the town centre. Llandrindod lies on the A483 between Builth Wells and New Radnor.

St Thomas' Chapel, LUDLOW

(SO 508 747)

Almost nine hundred years ago the ruthless, grasping Norman earl Roger de Lacy began construction of a powerful stone fortress to enforce his hold on the territory surrounding his seat at Ludlow. Virtually all of the earl's stronghold remains to be seen today, Ludlow being one of the few eleventh-century stone castles built in Britain which has survived more-or-less intact. A fortified town was also established here, to bring some measure of economic stability to the area, and the spiritual needs of the townsfolk were served by the parish church. Just within the walls, on the steep road down to Ludford Bridge (where, in 1459, one of the battles of the Wars of the Roses was fought) stands a lesser-known survivor of medieval Ludlow. Indeed, this is one of the oldest buildings in the town, yet strangely enough it seldom receives more than a passing mention in any guidebook. This is the chapel of St Thomas the Martyr, and was established a few years after Thomas à Becket's wretched death in Canterbury in 1170.

The obvious remains form only part of a larger structure, for half the chapel has been turned into a private dwelling house. Large arches in the north and west walls led into a now demolished nave and transept, and although the original vaulting has gone the slender rib-moulding survives, supporting a modern timber roof. The chapel apparently had a cruciform plan when it was first built, but alterations carried out in the eighteenth century totally transformed the original layout.

St Thomas' chapel lies in the shadow of the great castle, a site few visitors to Ludlow would miss. Inside the castle walls there is another ruined chapel which is worth a brief mention. This is St Mary Magdalene's chapel, arguably the most outstanding example of castle-chapels in Britain. The rich diversity of stone carvings will no doubt surprise many visitors, but what is even more astonishing about the chapel is its shape – for St Mary's is round! The apsidal chancel has vanished, leaving the circular nave standing alone, offering the visitor some fine examples of the glories of Romanesque architecture.

Access:
Both castle and chapel are freely accessible. Ludlow town lies on the A49 between Shrewsbury and Hereford.

The surviving rib-moulding of the chancel vault at St Thomas' chapel, Ludlow

St Mary's Church, NEWTOWN

(SO 108 918)

Booming Newtown has grown beyond the confines of the small settlement established here on the banks of the Severn during the Middle Ages. Two relics of the town's historic past have only barely survived the centuries: on private land just outside the town stands the overgrown mound of a Welsh or Norman castle; and more striking is the roofless shell of the old parish church of St Mary. It is a large but plain late-medieval building, noteworthy for its timber belfry – still intact – which is a characteristic feature of certain borderland churches.

In 1847 a new parish church was built at the opposite end of the town, on a site less prone to flooding, and the elaborate fifteenth-century wooden screen was salvaged from the demolished building and used to line the walls of the new chancel. The then rector, T.L.L. Williams, wrote:

St Mary's church, Newtown. Robert Owen's tomb can be seen in the foreground

portions of the old rood screen have been made use of . . . for the decoration of the chancel of the parish church. The panels of the screen have been put together in such a way that if at any time it is thought possible to make use of them for a screen they can easily be taken from the position in which they are now placed.

The rector also observed that the 'ancient font of the parish had been allowed to go out of keeping of the church authorities'. It was later restored to the new church, where it can be seen today. The stone bowl is octagonal in shape and probably dates to the fifteenth century.

In 1909 the parish holy well was still in existence, but because the poor people of the parish used to draw the water for their domestic needs, it was visited by the Sanitary Inspectors who declared it to be a health hazard and filled it in. Fortunately the old church was saved such an indifferent fate, and in 1939 a local commission was formed to clean up the area and keep the ruins in a tidy condition. It is now a pleasant and peaceful place. The ruined south walls have been used as flower beds, so that in spring and summer blossoming colours bring life to the cold stone. There is a central grass lawn, surrounded by a cobbled walkway lined by neat ranks of displaced eighteenth- and nineteenth-century memorial slabs. One poignant, if somewhat awkward, verse commemorates young Elizabeth Breeze, who died in 1819 aged twelve:

> All you that's young
> Behold and see
> How quietly death
> Has conquered me

A more incongruous addition to the ruined church is a small, free-standing 'chapel' at the east end, which looks like a medieval 'Wendy House' but is, in fact, a memorial of *c.* 1900 to the Pryce family of Newtown Hall. The oddest member of this ancient family was Sir John, who died in 1761: he kept the embalmed bodies of his deceased wives in his bedroom (much to the annoyance of his third wife, who demanded their removal)!

Newtown old church is perhaps better known as the final resting place of Robert Owen, the philanthropist and Utopian socialist, who was born in this town in 1771. Owen was a pioneer of factory reform in the early nineteenth century, and was hailed as the father of distributive co-operation. He was also the founder of nursery schools, both here and in the towns and cities of the northern United Kingdom, for the children of factory workers – a ray of light in the contemporary darkness of Welsh rural education. Owen died in 1858 and his monumental tomb, enclosed by stout iron bars, stands against the bare walls of the empty church. Emblazoned on the side are his words, full of Victorian idealism: 'It is the one great and universal interest of the Human race to be cordially united and to aid each other to the full extent of their capacities.'

Access:
Freely accessible. The church lies at the north end of town beside the River Severn. It can be reached from the main street or along a path from the riverside car-park. Newtown is situated on the A483 between Welshpool and Llanidloes.

Ednol Chapel, OLD RADNOR
(SO 233 648)

The lost chapel of Ednol lies in an upland district of the old county of Radnorshire, an area aptly, if somewhat harshly, described by one church historian as

> a mountainous tract, inhospitable and bleak ... the churches [here] are rarely placed within a village, they are rather the centre of a scattered district, sometimes standing alone, but with a grass track from the road to the church.

In the case of Ednol, remoter than most, this proved to be the cause of its downfall, and now the crumbling foundations of this hillside shrine are trampled by the feet of itinerant sheep. A grove of elder trees stand guard over the lost chapel, the twisted branches framing a magnificent view north-east over the rolling Radnorshire countryside to the English midlands.

Only mounds and tumbled stonework remain to be seen at the site of Ednol chapel

Unlike the view, the remains of this building are less than impressive, but the stony earthworks of a plain, rectangular structure can easily be made out in the cropped grass. The surviving wall faces are composed of a thin, slatey stone, and a slight depression in the south-western corner probably indicates the position of the entrance.

Ednol was the chapel-of-ease for the medieval borough of Old Radnor, down in the valley below. Services were held here until the 1820s, after which time the church was abandoned. When the Royal Commission on Ancient and Historical Monuments surveyed the building in 1911, only the lower walls and some timber fragments remained. Two of the fragments were oak roof beams, while another was part of a screen which separated the chancel from the nave. The few surviving timber screens at churches such as Llananno, Beguildy and Old Radnor display the magnificence of late-medieval craftsmanship which must once have graced this little upland chapel.

Access:
On private land, although a public footpath crosses the site. At the

Kinnerton crossroad on the B4372, New Radnor road, take the left-hand turn and proceed along this road for about 1½ miles. Just past Ednol farm there is a sharp bend in the road, and a gate on the left opens on to the short path leading up to the chapel site.

Poynton Chapel

(SJ 570 178)

No signpost points the way to Poynton chapel, nor is there a plaque to commemorate its presence. Anyone travelling the narrow, twisting lanes between the sleepy Shropshire villages of Roden and Shawbury will have to look long and hard at the many roadside farm buildings to identify this site; for Poynton chapel has shed its ecclesiastical garb and is now disguised as a humble stable. All that remains of the medieval building is the east gable wall, with its resplendent Perpendicular window enriched with decorative tracery. The carefully shaped blocks of grey stone contrast with the rugged red brickwork and timber framing of a post-Reformation stable which was built up against the surviving wall after the destruction of the chapel.

The Saxon manor of 'Peventone' is listed in the Domesday survey of 1086, and by the thirteenth century it was held by the De Peninton family. But the earliest known evidence to suggest the existence of a chapel at the manor occurs in the parish register of 1328, which records the death of the rector. His successor, Richard de Brewood, died in 1349, possibly a victim of the plague. Parish records of baptisms, weddings and funerals indicate that the little chapel was in use up to the seventeenth century. In 1611 the last recorded baptism was carried out 'in the newe fonte of Poynton Chapple', and the records' subsequent silence perhaps indicates that the unsettled religious and social conditions preceding the Civil War period signalled the downfall of this rural shrine.

Although parish documents hint that there was a chapel here at least by 1328, the surviving fragments of stonework are much later in date. This indicates probable rebuilding on the site of an older structure, in

The wall of a cowshed now boasts the medieval east gable of the former chapel at Poynton

the latter part of the fifteenth century. The adjacent timber-framed sixteenth-century manor house was once the home of the sheriffs of Shropshire, who no doubt once worshipped at this chapel. But now the congregation has been replaced by farm animals, and the fate of this rural chapel has been aptly summed up by the local historian, J.A. Morris, in his *History of Poynton Chapel*: 'unlike Bethlehem, which was first a stable and then became a Shrine, Poynton was first a Shrine and is now a stable.'

Access:
On private land, but the exterior can be viewed from the roadside. It lies about 7 miles north-east of Shrewsbury, off the B5062 to High Ercall. Just before reaching the village of Roden turn left, and about half a mile along this road there is a sharp bend, and the chapel will be seen on the left.

Shobdon Arches

(SO 401 629)

Visitors to Shobdon will no doubt agree that this 'lost' church is one of the oddest sites in Britain. For the medieval stonework, resplendent with Romanesque carvings, was dismantled in the eighteenth century and reassembled on a nearby hilltop as a folly – or, more accurately, a 'viewstopper'. And it performs this task admirably today. Who can fail to be intrigued by the bizarre 'arches' set at the far end of a long avenue of trees, along which the eye is irresistibly drawn? Many follies were built in the style of ancient buildings, but few actually used old masonry to such dramatic effect.

The church was built in the early twelfth century by Oliver de Merlimond, chief steward to the Mortimer lords of Wigmore Castle, and the lavish decorative style used by the builders has since become

A detail from one of the weathered carvings of Shobdon Arches

The re-erected arches of the demolished church

known as the Herefordshire or 'Kilpeck School'. Indeed, a visit to the famous church at Kilpeck, 8 miles south-west of Hereford, will give the visitor some idea of the almost overwhelming glories of this architectural style. The arches display convoluted and confusing tangles of birds, beasts, knights, saints, chevrons, knot-work and dragons belching fire. The doorways, topped by massive tympanum slabs, are carved with scenes depicting Christ in Majesty and the Harrowing of Hell. Celtic and Scandinavian influences have been detected in the sculptures, but Spanish designs have also been recognized, and since De Merlimond had travelled through France and Spain on a pilgrimage to Compostella he may have wanted to create a church on a par with majestic continental shrines.

De Merlimond's architectural masterpiece survived until 1746, when it was decided to rebuild, rather than repair, the Norman church. The owner of the surrounding estate, Lord Bateman, removed the doorways and internal arches and created his own architectural curiosity, much as De Merlimond had done centuries before. Unfortunately the medieval masons had chosen a soft red sandstone with which to demonstrate their skills, so that today, after centuries of exposure to the elements, the carvings are badly weathered. What was once hailed as a 'conservative measure that does Lord Bateman credit' is now deplored. Recently however, English Heritage have been debating the best way to conserve the arches. They considered five possibilities, including their removal, but it seems likely that the arches will be preserved *in situ* within a huge glass pyramid. The pyramid would have a door, enabling visitors to enter the structure for a closer look at the carvings. This idea, if carried to fruition, will be a startling advancement in the preservation of ancient monuments in this country – all that is now needed is the estimated £150,000 to construct it!

Access:

The arches stand on the hill overlooking an ornamental lake at Shobdon Court, just north of the parish church. The remains are accessible to the public and can be reached along a footpath from the church, where there is limited parking space. Shobdon lies on the B4362 between Presteigne and Mortimer's Cross.

Urishay Chapel

(SO 323 376)

The long scenic drive from Peterchurch in Golden Valley to Urishay in the hills above allows the visitor to glimpse more than geographical changes. The gleaming half-timbered farmhouses give way to more robust stone dwellings, and the woods thin as the heights of Urishay Common are reached.

Approaching the crest of a hill, you catch a fleeting glimpse of the shattered walls and tottering chimneys of Urishay 'Castle' through a screen of trees on the left. Here too stands the old chapel, looking more like a disused farm building than a former place of worship. Half the chapel is unroofed and unsafe, the leaning walls propped up with makeshift scaffolding, but there is some hope for this forgotten ruin. Plans are in hand to carry out a programme of restoration work, and part of the building has already been re-roofed.

The interior of the chapel is dark, dusty and echoing. The monotony of the plain, slaty stonework is relieved only by the massive wooden roof timbers and a modern beam which replaces the vanished chancel arch. At the time of our visit a house martin had built a nest in a nook under the rafters, and the scrawny fledgelings were indifferently fouling the massive stone altar beneath. Although some features, such as windows and the south doorway, date the building to the sixteenth and seventeenth centuries, two surviving doorways and a window have rounded heads, indicating a much earlier date, possibly twelfth-century.

Urishay chapel was undoubtedly the private place of worship for the Norman lords of the adjacent motte and bailey stronghold. Indeed, the building sits uncomfortably close to the marshy ditch encircling the mound. From the timber keep which originally crowned the summit, the warrior-landowners could keep a watchful eye on their domain, ever vigilant against the threat of a Welsh uprising from the mountainous lands not far to the west. All the medieval features of the castle apart from the earthworks were swept away in the seventeenth century when a large stone hall was built on top of the flattened mound. The cold fireplaces, fallen beams and ragged window openings which peer from the crumbling walls all serve to enhance the melancholy atmosphere of the place. The building was still occupied until the First World

War when, it is said, an ex-soldier member of the family squandered away the ancestral riches. A prized collection of books was sold and taken to Kansas, USA. The owners of the adjacent farm recall a vague tradition that Urishay Castle, like all self-respecting ruins, is haunted – though by what or whom no one knows!

Access:
The chapel is freely accessible and can be reached from the roadside via a gate and short path. Urishay lies on the west side of Golden Valley and can be reached from the B4348 along a signposted road.

Aberllynfi Chapel
(SO 172 380)

Aberllynfi was home to the deposed Welsh rulers of the area after its conquest by the Normans, and was the only untithed parish in Breconshire. Bernard Newmarch invaded Breconshire in 1093, and slew its rightful owner Bleddyn ap Maenarch. Anxious to cultivate the good will of the Welsh population, he conferred Aberllynfi on Bleddyn's eldest son, Gwrgan, and so a powerful dynasty took control of the area. Nothing remains today to mark the site of the castle of these Welsh magnates except a large mound. Near to it are the remains of the church, which fell into disuse during the latter half of the seventeenth century. Marriages and baptisms here are recorded up to 1695, and in 1698 the church saw the burial of one Charles Prichard of Pipton who was reputedly 110 years old when he died. Today only a few remnants of walling remain to be seen.

There is a grim anecdote relating to the abandonment of the church, recounted by an elderly inhabitant of the parish in the early part of this century. A duel is said to have taken place in the church one Sunday morning between two claimants to a neighbouring estate. The duel resulted in the death of one of the protagonists, and thereafter the church was never used for religious service.

Access:
On private land, although the castle earthworks can be seen from the roadside. The church site lies in a field behind Three Cocks village, on the A438 Brecon to Leominster road, about 3 miles north-east of Talgarth.

All Saints Church,
BROCKHAMPTON-BY-ROSS
(SO 598 317)

The building of a new parish church at Brockhampton-by-Ross in 1902 signalled the end for the humble, dilapidated medieval building which had for so long served the spiritual needs of the parishioners. Today the church of All Saints is a roofless ruin in the grounds of Brockhampton Court Hotel. It was probably built early in the fifteenth century, a date suggested by the few surviving Perpendicular windows – although the massive western tower (which occupies the whole width of the building) was raised in the following century. Services at All Saints were discontinued in the 1930s and the passing years have greatly affected the building. Unlike many of the other 'replacement' churches, the 1902 building is more distinguished than its predecessor: it has a concrete vaulted roof (a curious blend of ancient techniques and modern materials) and tapestries designed by the Pre-Raphaelite artist Burne-Jones.

Access:
On private land in the grounds of the Court Hotel, Brockhampton village. The village overlooks the River Wye, just off the B4224 Ross-on-Wye to Hereford road.

St John's Church, YAZOR

(SO 404 465)

The old parish church of St John at Yazor is one of those unfortunate sites where only part of the building has been retained for ecclesiastical use, the remainder being allowed to fall into decay. The churchyard is approached along a farm track, guarded by soldierly ranks of young yew trees. A far older specimen beside the church has a remarkable appearance, for its massive trunk has been split apart by some cataclysm, and from the hollow centre a new tree has grown.

In 1855 a replacement church was built some distance away, and most of the old St John's demolished apart from the tower and south transept. A few years later the transept was repaired for use as a small chapel, but today it is little used and is becoming increasingly dilapidated. Prior to demolition the church consisted of a nave and chancel (both gone), a south aisle (one arch alone remains) and a transept, all dating probably to *c.* 1300. The ruin of a tower also remains: a massive, monolithic structure, now entirely swathed in vegetation. It is remarkable that this has survived at all, for the foundations must have been poorly laid; five great butresses have been built against the outer walls to prop up the tottering structure.

Access:
Freely accessible, and reached through a farmyard just off the A480 Kington road, 8 miles north-west of Hereford.

CHESTER AND NORTH-EAST WALES

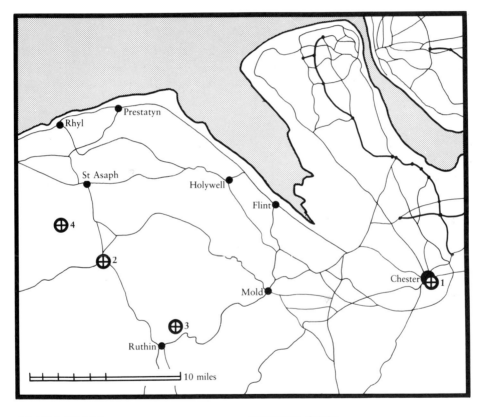

MAIN SITES

1. *St John's Church, Chester*
2. *St Hilary's Chapel and Leicester's Church, Denbigh*
3. *St Peter's Church, Llanbedr-dyffryn-Clwyd*

LESSER SITE

4. *Ffynnon Fair, Cefn*

St John's Church, CHESTER

(SJ 409 661)

St John's church in Chester is perhaps the finest example included here of sites where part of the building is still in religious use. Its origins date back to the Dark Ages, when the Saxons established a church outside the great ruined Roman city of 'Deva', headquarters of the XXth legion.

Nothing now survives of that building for, like the nearby cathedral, the arrival of the Normans in the late eleventh century brought architectural as well as sociological changes. With the creation of the earldom of Chester in 1081 the old Anglo-Saxon centre was rebuilt as a seat of Norman power and authority. From their fortress on the edge of the Dee the earls of Chester ruled like kings in their palatinate, using the city as a base for conquest further west.

Their energies were not, however, solely engaged in war-like activities, and St John's is only one of a legacy of many fine buildings left by the Norman conquerors. It is built, like most of Chester's buildings, from a locally quarried red sandstone, a richly coloured rock which glows in the light of the setting sun and which is so easily shaped by the elements. The ruined part of the building is that of the transepts and chancel – which retain, however, their noble, ponderous Norman arches and blind arcades. The more pointed arches are innovations from the fourteenth century. To the west the nave is blocked off from the chancel. Here, inside the gloomy, echoing nave one can see the splendour that was lost when the church was truncated: the solid, cumbersome, Norman arcade, austerely beautiful in its strength and simplicity; faded traces of wall paintings on the pillars; a roof of later date, almost lost in the darkness above; and the eye is drawn ever onwards to the chancel and high altar, now a mouldering ruin in the graveyard outside.

This was the original Norman cathedral of Mercia, established by Bishop Peter some five hundred years before the Abbey of St Werburgh became the new cathedral at the Reformation. It is said to have been founded by King Ethelred in the seventh century, but is more likely to have been built by King Alfred's daughter Aethelfreda, who restored and rebuilt the 'City of Legions' in AD 907.

The ruined east end of the chapel of St John's, Chester

The cathedral status of St John's was short lived, for Bishop Peter's successor moved the see to Lichfield in 1102. It became a collegiate church until the Dissolution of the Monasteries in 1536, after which the nave was then used by the townsfolk for worship. The tower at the north-west end of the nave collapsed in 1573 and was then rebuilt, but collapsed again in 1881; it has since been left as a ruin. A rather interesting facet of the church's history occurred in 1573, when Elizabeth I gave the building to the parishioners, in return for some roof lead to be used for shot. It was then that the east end of the building was sealed off, leaving the choir and Lady chapel to crumble into ruin.

Access:
The ruined part of St John's is not accessible to the public, although the remains can be seen from the surrounding parkland. The church lies off Vicar's Lane beyond the Roman amphitheatre at Newgate, Chester.

St Hilary's Chapel & Leicester's Church, DENBIGH

(SJ 053 659)

The medieval town of Denbigh sprawls atop an isolated hill of limestone; a natural fortress designed by nature and improved by man. Five centuries ago, when the townsfolk were weary of being exposed to winter storms and hostile attacks, the old congested town was abandoned for a new commercial centre further north. Today ruins are more plentiful than inhabited buildings within the shattered walls of the ancient borough, and chief among them is the castle. This huge baronial stronghold was built by Henry de Lacy, Earl of Lincoln, in the aftermath of a Welsh rebellion in 1282. There is a story that the earl failed to finish building the castle, losing heart when his eldest son fell into the well and died.

Barely a stone's throw from the outer gatehouse is the surviving tower of St Hilary's chapel which, until a new church was built in 1874, remained as the only medieval building still to be used for its original purpose. St Hilary's was a dependant of the old Welsh foundation of Llanfarchell in the valley below, and was built *c.* 1300, in what was then an area of the walled town. In the turbulent and unsettled years of the fifteenth century, Denbigh town was burnt to the ground on two occasions, and by the end of the fifteenth century the old hilltop centre had apparently been abandoned. The chapel continued in use up until 1923, when most of the structure was demolished. Only the three-storeyed tower survives, with a short length of the nave wall. There was a long chancel with a crypt beneath, and a north aisle, which was probably a fifteenth-century addition and which was rebuilt in the eighteenth century.

A short distance downhill lie the remains of Leicester's church, named after its founder, Robert Dudley, Earl of Leicester, who began its construction in 1578. It is the only large Protestant church to have been built in Britain during the Elizabethan period. Dudley was Lord of Denbigh from 1563 to 1588, and embarked on his ambitious building scheme possibly in an attempt to replace the old cathedral at St Asaph. Whatever his motives, the project was never completed owing to lack of money, and the building is now a hollow shell with rows of spacious windows.

There is one other ruined site in Denbigh which deserves a brief mention, and that is the austere remains of the thirteenth-century Carmelite friary, located just outside the town on the St Asaph road.

Access:
All three sites are freely accessible and are in the care of CADW: Welsh Historic Monuments. Denbigh town lies off the A525 between Ruthin and St Asaph in the Vale of Clwyd.

St Peter's Church, LLANBEDR-DYFFRYN-CLWYD

(SJ 146 598)

From the ruined walls of Llanbedr, the expanse of the fertile Vale of Clwyd stretches away to the north and south, sandwiched between the Clwydian Hills and the Denbigh moors which form a dramatic backdrop to the landscape. This dominating viewpoint is reflected in the place-name, which means 'St Peter's church in the Vale of Clwyd'.

On approaching the church from the medieval borough of Ruthin,

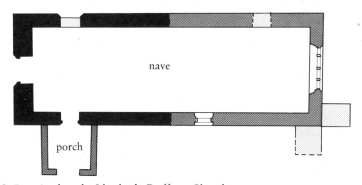

Plan of St Peter's church, Llanbedr-Dyffryn-Clwyd

The bell-cote at Llanbedr-Dyffryn-Clwyd is an incongruous modern addition

the tall bell-coted west end can be seen rising out of a thicket of greenery, which if left unchecked will soon completely obscure the ruin from view. The encircling churchyard is over-burdened with nettles, cow parsley and wood garlic, while the undergrowth busily engulfs the interior. There are two raised platforms inside the church, which can prove dangerous to the unwary explorer as they are not always visible. The main feature of the church, one which immediately captures the attention, is the ugly modern bell-cote on the west gable: it is an unsympathetic structure of grey stone, which clashes vehemently with the softer red sandstone of the original walls. All the early masonry, which dates to the thirteenth or fourteenth century, is easily distinguishable through the use of the local sandstone, a material which is easy to carve but is notoriously prone to weathering; the stone crumbles at the slightest touch.

The cluster of three doors at the west end of the building is unusual, perhaps extravagant, but there is little sign that they were later additions, as may have been expected. Half-way along the nave, the red walls give way to grey stone, clearly indicating that the eastern part of the church is a later extension, probably of the late fifteenth or early sixteenth century. There are signs of further additions, including two large and cumbersome buttresses on the south-east corner which were built to prop up the crumbling walls.

In 1863 a more conveniently sited church was built in the village, and old Llanbedr was left to decay; a process which has been exacerbated in recent years by neglect and fast-encroaching undergrowth. Photographs taken by the Royal Commission on Ancient and Historical Monuments in the early 1950s show the vanished south porch to have been a half-timbered structure with a remarkably ornate roof, carved with human figures and lion heads. No doubt the main roof of the church was as richly decorated. The chancel was formerly dominated by a large and elaborate Perpendicular east window. This too has been lost; all that now survives to remind us of Llanbedr's former splendour are a few carved fragments of stone heaped against the churchyard wall.

Access:
Llanbedr lies 2 miles north-east of Ruthin, off the A494.
Approaching from that direction, once in the village turn left past the

church, and then take the next right along a narrow lane. The old church will be seen in the trees on the right, and a gate in the field marks the start of a footpath.

Ffynnon Fair, CEFN
(SJ 032 709)

The very location of this well-chapel was instrumental in its downfall, for it is situated in the verdant, isolated valley of the river Elwy, some distance from the nearest settlement or road. According to the Revd Elias Owen, who made a study of Welsh well-chapels in the last century, the spring itself was probably enclosed originally in a small stone-walled baptistry, which later became the southern transept of a larger chapel. If this is true, then the enlargement of the building into a chapel is surely indicative of its former popularity. This is further evidenced by the construction of another well-chamber at the west end, but it is not certain if this was ever incorporated within the actual structure of the chapel. It was probably unroofed, with adjoining chambers where those seeking the curative properties of the spring could undress before immersing themselves in the cold, rushing waters.

The Reformation undoubtedly signalled the end for Ffynnon Fair, and by the late eighteenth century it was in decay – as the topographer, naturalist and diarist Thomas Pennant tells us:

> Ffynnon Fair, Our Lady's Well, a fine spring, inclosed in an angular wall formerly roofed, and the ruins of a cross-shaped chapel, finely overgrown with ivy . . . and this in days of pilgrimage, the frequent haunt of devotees.

There is sadly even less to see today, although some walls remain standing, and the overgrown spring still rises in its stone basin. The few surviving details indicate a late fifteenth-century date, and the chapel was probably erected on the plan of (and in rivalry with) the better-known St Winifred's well-chapel at nearby Holywell.

Today the ruins stand forlorn and neglected, imprisoned behind rusting iron railings, and totally overgrown with brambles and ivy. For the latter-day pilgrim there is little left to see, in sad contrast with the late-medieval splendours of Holywell, only 12 miles away on the Flint road.

Access:
On private land and not normally accessible. The chapel lies on the banks of the Elwy, off the B5381, 2 miles south-west of St Asaph.

GWYNEDD

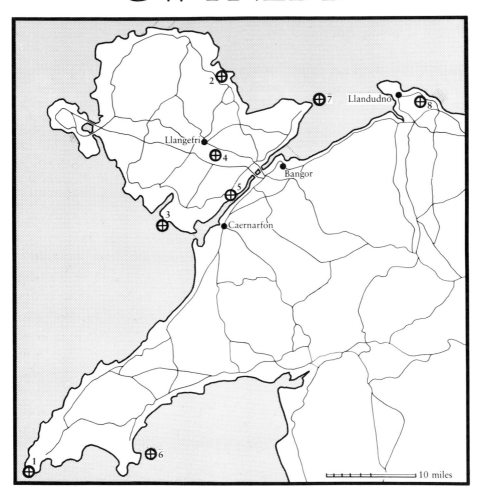

MAIN SITES

1. *Capel Fair, Aberdaron*
2. *Capel Lligwy, Anglesey*
3. *Llanddwyn Island, Anglesey*
4. *Llanfihangel Esgeifiog, Anglesey*
5. *Llanidan, Anglesey*
6. *St Tudwal's Island, Abersoch*

LESSER SITES

7. *Puffin Island, Anglesey*
8. *St Mary's Chapel, Penrhyn*

142

Capel Fair, ABERDARON

(SH 139 253)

Mynydd Mawr is the Land's End of North Wales, where the rocky headland plunges dramatically into the turbulent waters of Bardsey Sound. From the car-park at the end of the Aberdaron road a public footpath leads down to the coast, passing the site of Capel Fair, St Mary's Chapel. All that remains of the building today is a grass-grown mound within a large square enclosure. The site is best seen from higher ground to the north, especially when the sun is at a low angle and highlighting the earthworks. Also dedicated to St Mary is a curious holy well in a gully below the chapel. At low tide the sea reveals a natural rock basin in the side of the cliff which, remarkably, contains a spring of fresh water. Take a sip from the well and climb back up the steep hillside to the chapel: local legend maintains that if you succeed in reaching the top without dribbling your wish will be granted!

In full view from the headland is the brooding mass of Ynys Enlli – Bardsey Island – a mysterious, sacred place, long renowned as the burial site of twenty thousand saints. A Celtic monastery was established here in the Dark Ages and later an Augustinian abbey, but only two cross-stones and the crumbling tower of the abbey church remain. Nervous pilgrims bound for the island embarked from the mainland at Aberdaron, having first offered up a heartfelt prayer for a safe crossing at Capel Fair.

The nineteenth-century topographer Samuel Lewis briefly mentioned the old chapel, together with another ruined holy building 'called Capel Anhaelog, which . . . has been suffered, since the dissolution of Bardsey monastery, to fall into decay'. The remains of this building have long been razed to the ground, but two early Christian inscribed stones were moved from there to Cefnamlwch House, where they now rest. Both stones commemorate fifth-or sixth-century priests, one of whom is stated to lie 'with the multitude of the brethren', perhaps a reference to the countless holy men and devout pilgrims interred on the windswept, sea-ringed rock of Enlli.

Access:
Freely accessible. The chapel lies on National Trust property at the end of the Aberdaron to Llanllawen road, at the furthermost tip of the Lleyn Peninsula.

Capel Lligwy, ANGLESEY
(SH 497 864)

The parish of Penrhos Lligwy occupies part of the rocky north-east coast of Anglesey, an area renowned not only for its coastal scenery but also for its legacy of ancient monuments, reflecting the long history of man on this island. Some five thousand years ago the Stone Age farmers of Penrhos constructed what might be regarded as both a 'parish' church and a sepulchre – a massive burial chamber or 'cromlech', fashioned from the many limestone slabs which outcrop in the vicinity. The same quarries also supplied the raw materials for the building of a settlement which was founded by a native clan at the time of the Roman occupation of Britain in the fourth century. Perhaps the inhabitants of this vanished community remain here in spirit, but only the monolithic slabs and foundations of roofless huts can be seen today.

Bleached limestone walls are all that survive of Capel Lligwy too. This medieval gesture of Christian power in a land so obviously imbued with the spirit of a pagan past was constructed many centuries after the prehistoric architectural ventures were in ruins. Now the wheel has turned full circle and Capel Lligwy today is just another ruined relic of a former age.

The chapel stands on a low, grassy hill, within sight of the sea, and is enclosed by a low stone wall within which a few skeletal bushes stand guard. It is a simple, square building of early twelfth-century date with a 'Norman' round-headed doorway – although the building was undoubtedly built by Welsh craftsmen under the patronage of the native princes of Gwynedd. An almost indistinguishable change in the character of the masonry suggests that the upper part of the walls were rebuilt in the later Middle Ages. In the early sixteenth century a small

The diminutive twelfth-century ruin of Capel Lligwy, with its sixteenth-century side-chapel

and ruggedly austere south chapel was added to the chancel, from which a flight of slippery steps leads down into a dark vault roofed over with massive stone slabs – almost in imitation of the ancient burial chambers which dot the surrounding landscape.

Access:
In the care of CADW: Welsh Historic Monuments and freely accessible. The chapel lies about 1 mile east of Moelfre on the east coast of Anglesey. From Menai Bridge follow the A5025 through Benllech to the new roundabout. Take the second turning off this roundabout and continue along the road (passing the Lligwy burial chamber) for about a mile. There is some parking space, and the church can be reached by a path on the left. Follow this path beyond the chapel to the hut settlement of Din Lligwy.

Llanddwyn Island, ANGLESEY

(SH 387 627)

Llanddwyn is only an island at high tide, when the rushing waters of Caernarfon Bay cut off access from the mainland; but at most times of the day this promontory, jutting out like a long finger of rock into the sea, can easily be reached across the golden sands of Malltraeth Bay. This is arguably the most spectacular setting of all the lost churches included in this book. On a clear day the views from the island are breathtaking, with the mountainous backdrop of Snowdonia and the saw-toothed skyline of the Lleyn peninsula stretching away to the south. This headland now forms part of the Newborough Warren Nature Reserve, and there are discreetly sited car-parks with facilities, forestry walks and miles of unpolluted beaches, in this popular area of Anglesey.

It was the glorious view from Llanddwyn Island which no doubt inspired the legend of St Dwynwen's death. As she lay dying, Dwynwen requested to be taken to see the sun set below the watery horizon one last time. She was carried as far as the shelter of a great boulder, which miraculously split apart for Dwynwen's last glimpse of that which she thought so beautiful. The cliff-edge boulder is still there, complete with its curious 'spy-hole'. Another of the great rocks which pierce the grassy shroud of the island has a curious power associated with it: the bed-like slab, known as *Gwely Esyth*, was believed to cure rheumatism, and those afflicted would sleep on it, then awake and cut their names into the surrounding turf. They would leave the island secure in the belief that they were cured.

St Dwynwen built her oratory and hermitage on this remote island in the century following the Roman retreat from Britain. She became one of the more appealing of the Dark Age saints, and tradition holds that she came to this site because she had been crossed in love. Thereafter she became renowned as the patron saint of lovers, a Welsh 'Valentine', and the power of her sacred well on Llanddwyn enabled pilgrims to ascertain the faithfulness of their chosen ones. The ritual was complicated and hinged on the behaviour of an eel which lived in the well. Breadcrumbs were sprinkled on the water and then covered over with a piece of cloth or a handkerchief. If the eel took the cloth down along with

Llanddwyn: the island ruins of 'St Dwynwen's abbey'

the crumbs, then it was a sign that the pilgrim's loved one was unfaithful.

The habit of consulting the oracular eel has, not surprisingly, waned, and the well is now an inconspicuous marshy hollow. Nothing remains of St Dwynwen's Dark Age shrine, and the stark ruins which now dominate the central part of the island belong to a church built here a few decades before the Reformation, in the early sixteenth century. This was a comparatively large building of cruciform plan, with a chancel, nave, stair turret and twin transepts. Even though centuries of wind and rain have reduced the building mostly to foundations, the plan can still be traced. The chancel is the most substantial part of the ruin, with three ragged openings in the crumbling walls marking the site of spacious windows. In the long grass nearby are tumbled fragments of carved stones which hint at the vanished architectural splendour of the building. In contrast to the roomy chancel the nave is disproportionately small and may, in fact, be all that survives of the pre-Tudor building. Mounds and irregularities in the tussocky ground mark the remains of an encircling churchyard.

The nineteenth-century historian Richard Fenton recounted a belief that the church had been in ruins for about two hundred years (that is, from around 1600), and at the beginning of the eighteenth century more of the building remained to be seen. Henry Rowlands, Vicar of Llanidan, wrote:

> in the middle of this peninsula, on a pleasant and open spot of level ground . . . lies the church, of melancholy appearance, stripped of its roof, and doomed to fall into ruin from the destructive effects of age. The Prebendary's House . . . is now altogether fallen down and a mass of ruins . . .

The scant remains of the priest's dwelling can be seen as an earthwork a short distance south of the church. Two modern Celtic crosses, some huddled cottages and a small lighthouse are also to be found on Llanddwyn Island, all adding to the romantic nature of the peninsula and encouraging belief in St Dwynwen as the patron saint of lovers.

Access:
The church ruins are freely accessible, though access to the island is restricted by high tide. Llanddwyn lies beyond Newborough Warren, where there is ample car-parking off a signposted minor road 2¼ miles south-west of Newborough.

Llanfihangel Esgeifiog, ANGLESEY
(SH 478 734)

Cradled in a grove of trees, and peering from behind the ruins of an abandoned farmstead, this site conjures up the more romantic aspect of a 'lost' church. Llanfihangel Esgeifiog is one of the most architecturally complex churches in Anglesey – and it is certainly the most overgrown! In summer the voracious undergrowth grips the ruined building in a stranglehold that only winter can loosen; it is often difficult to see where the greenery ends and the stonework begins. A visit to this church, which is dedicated to St Michael, is perhaps best in late autumn or early spring, when the encircling trees are aglow with russet leaves or bursting with fresh life.

This fifteenth-century doorway leads into the gloomy, overgrown interior of
Llanfihangel Esgeifiog

A short walk across a field brings the visitor to this little-known holy site, which, like the community who worshipped within it, has grown, flourished, declined and died. By the middle of the nineteenth century the church was in decay and in need of repair, but was still used by the dwindling congregation. But the population gradually shifted away from the old centre to the village of Gaerwen on the main Bangor to Holyhead road, a short distance further south. All the removable fittings were taken from the old church to a new building in the village, including a fourteenth-century bell inscribed with the name 'Michael'.

From the roadside an unmarked footpath leads west to the church, alongside a disused, sunken lane, now little more than a muddy rill used by sheep. The entrance is still through a wrought iron gate in the crumbling graveyard wall, which encloses and protects its forlorn inmate. Only a few headstones peering above the long grass and brambles serve to remind us of the long departed people who rest here.

All that now remains of St Michael's is a roofless, L-shaped building, approached through a finely carved fifteenth-century doorway. But look closely at the weathered stonework and you will see joints and abutments which reveal that the existing building is the result of many modifications. The original medieval church was probably a simple rectangular building comprising a nave and chancel. Then a south chapel was added, and a new east window inserted into the chancel at the end of the sixteenth century. Around 1638 a wealthy local family, the Hollands of Plas Berw, built the surviving north chapel, an event which is commemorated by an inscription above the gable window. With the change in population levels in the nineteenth century the church may have been considered too large, or in need of excessive repair, for the nave was entirely demolished apart from the salvaged fifteenth-century door which was set in the new end wall. The demolition of the south chapel around 1874 further reduced the building to its present stunted plan. The visitor who now enters this melancholy ruin stands in what is left of the chancel, in front of the high altar, that most sacred part of a medieval church.

Access:
St Michael's church lies on private land but can be reached by an unmarked public footpath. From the village of Pentre Berw on the

A5, 4 miles west of Menai Bridge, follow the road leading north-east to Ceint. About ¾ mile along this road, and before you reach a large farm set back off the road on the left, the church can just be glimpsed in the trees. A modern gate on the left marks the start of the path of Llanfihangel.

Llanidan, ANGLESEY

(SH 495 668)

Llanidan is a large straggling parish bordering the Menai Straits, within sight of the rugged peaks of Snowdon and the castellated town of Caernarfon. The surrounding landscape contains some of the finest monuments of ancient man in Anglesey; there is the dark and eerie burial chamber of Bryn-Celli-ddu, which was built around four millenia ago within an earlier 'henge'; two earthworks at Castell Bryngwyn and Caer Leb sheltered a farming community in the Iron Age and Roman periods; and beside the road at Bodowyr stands the skeleton of a Neolithic stone tomb. These so-called 'Druidical' monuments have long attracted the attention of antiquarians, including the eighteenth-century historian and rector of Llanidan, Henry Rowlands.

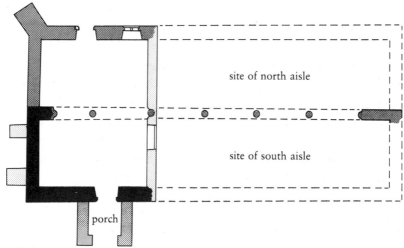

Plan of Llanidan old church

The church which Rowlands officiated in is now an evocative shell, decorously mantled with ivy and enclosed by an overgrown graveyard 'little occupied by the dead and little tended by the living'. Only about a third of the building retains its roof, but even this part is rarely used, and is now a dark, dusty and empty place.

Like all self-respecting Welsh churches, the origins of Llanidan are lost in the mists of antiquity. It is dedicated reputedly to a seventh-century bishop of Lindisfarne, St Aiden, but the existing masonry is unlikely to date from earlier than the fourteenth century. The only relic of an earlier church here is the stone font, richly carved with sinuous interlocking plant-forms, which is believed to be of late twelfth- or early thirteenth-century date. This is now kept in the new parish church at nearby Brynsiencyn village, which was built after the partial demolition of Llanidan in 1844. This event, prompted by the general decay of the medieval building, and by a shift in population, was criticized by the contemporary antiquarian H. Longeville Jones: 'In an evil hour the ruthless hand of the destroyer was allowed to be lifted against it.' Jones surveyed the truncated church and observed with bitter irony that the

Llanidan: the Perpendicular arches of the ruined church march off into the overgrown graveyard

most insecure part was that which had been preserved for future use! The rest of the building was knocked down except for the elegant Perpendicular arcade, which now rises from the graveyard like an abstract sculpture. The few surviving windows and doors show good examples of late-medieval stone carving, testifying to the vanished splendour of Llanidan.

All that remains of the earliest masonry is part of the south aisle. This is likely to have formed part of the original fourteenth-century nave, but towards the end of the fifteenth century, in the more settled times of the Tudor dynasty, the church was greatly enlarged and refurbished. A north aisle was built, and a vaulted south porch. The surviving part of the arch-braced timber roof is likely to date from this period of wholesale reconstruction.

The dark, damp interior contains many carved and inscribed stones, including an eighteenth-century sundial and two sixteenth-century heraldic plaques. One stone the visitor may have trouble finding is the magical *Maen Morddwydd* or 'stone of the thigh', so-called from its resemblance to a human thigh bone. It was more aptly known as the 'homing stone', for no matter how far away it was taken, it would always return to its original spot the following night. The ruthless Norman earl Hugh of Shrewsbury, doubting the folk-tales of credulous locals, chained the stone to a larger rock, and threw both into the sea. One can imagine the earl's astonishment when, on the following morning, the stone was back in its accustomed place. 'As a result the earl issued a public edict that no one . . . should be so presumptuous as to move it from its place', wrote the twelfth-century chronicler, Gerald of Wales. Gerald also noted that the stone was associated with darker, pre-Christian beliefs: if any couple risked making love near the stone ('which they do frequently', mutters Gerald) then the monolith would sweat great drops of water, and no child would be born from such a union. Even the inhabitants of a nearby cottage had abandoned their home, and a protective wall had been built around the stone.

From the legends surrounding it, the *Maen Morddwydd* may well have been one of the many Bronze Age standing stones which can be found on Anglesey. Gerald never mentioned where the stone was located, although later antiquarians, including Henry Rowlands, have linked it with Llanidan. Indeed Rowlands claimed it was built into the churchyard wall, 'but of late years [the stone] was pulled off and carried away'.

Access:
Freely accessible. Llanidan lies ½ mile east of Brynsiencyn along a signposted minor road which leaves the A4080 in the village.

St Tudwal's Island, ABERSOCH
(SH 342 259)

A mile or so out to sea beyond the summer tourist-trap of Abersoch can be seen two low-lying islands, the larger of which has formed a retreat and sanctuary for Celtic hermits since the Dark Ages. The importance of St Tudwal's Island has been overshadowed by the fame of Lleyn's other holy isle, *Ynys Enlli* (Bardsey), but St Tudwal's is the more archaeologically rewarding.

A conjectural reconstruction of the ecclesiastical settlement of St Tudwal's Island. The chapel and ancilliary buildings are shown on the right, with a fourteenth-century domestic hall on the left

An ecclesiastical settlement may have been established here in the sixth century by St Tudwal, although none of the surviving remains are as old as this. Excavations in 1959–61 revealed a complex of medieval buildings grouped about an early thirteenth-century church, set on the more sheltered east side of the island. During the thirteenth and fourteenth centuries additional buildings were constructed beside the little church, which was enlarged and provided with an adjoining sacristy. This thick-walled sacristy evidently had an upper floor, for a mass of stonework against the outer wall was interpreted by the excavators as the remains of a stairway. A large domestic hall of mid-fourteenth-century date was added on to one side of the courtyard.

For centuries the inhabitants of this remote island were Celtic monks or 'culdees', an Irish name meaning 'servants of God', but by the early fifteenth century the '*Prioris de Enys Tudwal*' had been conferred on the Augustinian order. The community lasted until the Dissolution of the Monasteries under Henry VIII, and when the King's antiquary, John Leland, passed through North Wales in *c.* 1540, he saw here only 'a litle chirche now desolute'. St Tudwal's was settled occasionally by pirates and farmers, and the ruinous church was rebuilt as a barn, but in 1887 a more determined effort was made to re-colonize the island. A Welsh Roman Catholic, Father Henry Hughes, attempted to revive the former monastic associations of the island by establishing a Dominican house there and, until his sudden death later that year, a small, dedicated community lived on St Tudwal's in tents and corrugated iron-roofed 'round huts'.

Access:
The island is private property and access – by boat – must be arranged from the harbour at Abersoch. St Tudwal's lies off the Lleyn coast about 6 miles south-west of Pwllheli.

Puffin Island, ANGLESEY
(SH 653 823)

Over the centuries Puffin Island has had many names, the present one being no more than a nickname. To the feared, sea-roving Vikings this whale-shaped limestone rock was known as Priestholm, and to the Welsh as *Ynys Lannog*, or *Ynys Seiriol*, the island of St Seiriol.

Seiriol was a sixth-century saint who founded both a monastery on the island, and one on the mainland at Penmon, where the austere, brooding, twelfth-century priory church stands close to the saint's holy well and primitive hut dwelling. He is said to have been related to Maelgwn Gwynedd, a Dark Age Celtic king, whose principal court was at Degannwy near Llandudno. In AD 632 Puffin Island entered recorded history when Cadwallon, king of Gwynedd and a descendant of Maelgwn, was besieged on the island by Edwin, king of Northumbria. This event, recorded in the medieval Welsh *Chronicles of the Princes*, is significant since it shows just how early the Anglo-Saxons had managed to penetrate into Wales.

During the twelfth century the rocky island was a hive of monastic activity; in fact it would have resembled a medieval version of the well-known Greek monastery on Mount Athos. Gerald of Wales writes of it as being 'inhabited by hermits who live in the service of God by the labour of their hands . . . many bodies of their saints are deposited there and no woman is allowed to enter the island'. Gerald also recounted a more tongue-in-cheek story about what would occur should the monks quarrel with each other:

> a species of small mice, which abound on the island, consume most of their food and drink, and befoul the rest. As soon as their argument is over, the plague of mice disappears immediately.

All that remains today of the early monastic settlement is a group of square dwelling huts, or cells, within a stone-walled enclosure, all ruined and partly obscured by the tussocky undergrowth. More obvious, and clearly visible from the mainland, is the monolithic tower of a twelfth-century church. This has three floors, rising to a height of 40 ft, and is surmounted by a pyramidal stone roof. In plan and detail it closely resembles the mother church at Penmon. Although nothing now survives of the nave and chancel, their roof-lines can be seen on the sides of the tower. There are also the ruins of a post-Reformation cottage. Today the island is uninhabited by man. There are gulls, guillemots, cormorants, puffins, rabbits and rats; the island abounds in these little creatures. Boat trips around Priestholm can be booked from

Llandudno, but the rats ensure that the monastic ruins rest in peace from the clatter of would-be pilgrims.

Access:
The island is privately owned and not normally accessible. It lies at the eastern-most point of Anglesey, beyond the Trwyn Du coastguard look-out station at Penmon. Penmon, with its fine Norman church, sixteenth-century dovecot and ancient holy well, can be reached from Beaumaris off the B5109.

St Mary's Chapel, PENRHYN
(SM 816 816)

Penrhyn is a village clustered about the beetling cliffs of the Little Ormes Head, midway between the twin tourist haunts of Llandudno and Colwyn Bay. There is still, however, an air of rural tranquillity about the area. The busy A546 takes its annual stream of visitors past within a stone's throw of St Mary's chapel, but few know of its existence. It lies at the rear of a small car-park, in a field opposite the '1590 Club'; an incongruous setting, yet the chapel is a delightful little building and well worth a visit.

In 1535 Penrhyn was described as *'libera Capella Beatae Mariae de Penrhyn'*, a royal chapel of St Mary, and half the tithes of Llandudno belonged to it. The Reformation had little effect on the chapel, and it was undoubtedly used as a private place of worship by the occupants of nearby Penrhyn Old Hall, a large and imposing sixteenth-century house. However, by the early nineteenth century it had been turned into a farm building, and remained in this less dignified service until it was restored to its religious purposes in *c.* 1930.

Today that restoration work has been undone, and neglect has reduced Penrhyn chapel to the status of a 'romantic ruin'. It is a simple rectangular building, constructed of limestone – no doubt quarried from the nearby outcrops. A contrasting red sandstone has been used for the corner-stones and windows. The date of the building is uncertain, for many original details have been lost during earlier

Cutaway reconstruction of St Mary's chapel, Penrhyn

restoration work, but it may have been built around 1500. There is a 'Tudor' doorway in the west wall, and above that a carved stone depicting Jesus and the two Marys. Inside, the tottering roof is still partly held up by two original arch-braced trusses, hung with curtains of ivy which drape the crumbling, plastered walls.

Access:
On private land, but visible from the roadside and car-park just west of the Penrhyn roundabout on the A546, 3 miles north-west of Colwyn Bay.

GLOSSARY

| | 5 feet |
| | 1.5 metres |

ARCHITECTURAL STYLES

NORMAN (*c.* 1060–*c.* 1200)

Chancel arch, Runston

The earliest phase of medieval architecture, also known as 'Romanesque' from the Roman use of rounded arches. This style is characterized by massive pillars, round-headed doors and windows, often with chevron carvings. Edvin Loach, Runston and Shobdon are good examples of the Norman style.

EARLY ENGLISH (*c.* 1180–*c.* 1280)

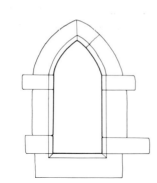

Window, Eccleswall Court

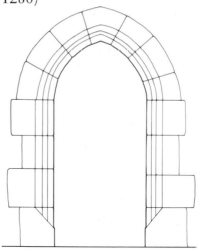

Doorway, Llanbedr-Dyffryn-Clwyd

This is the earliest phase of English 'Gothic' architecture, less ponderous than Norman, with slender pillars and window openings with pointed heads and simple tracery. St Hilary's at Denbigh, Llanbedr and Eccleswall Court display examples of Early English architecture.

DECORATED (*c.* 1270–*c.* 1380)

Two-light window, Llanwarne

This style gradually succeeded the Early English in the fourteenth century, and is characterized by a greater emphasis on fine detail, such as foliage carvings on the tops of pillars, and elaborate tracery in window heads. Llanwarne is an outstanding example of both Early English *and* Decorated architecture.

PERPENDICULAR (*c.* 1380–*c.* 1550)

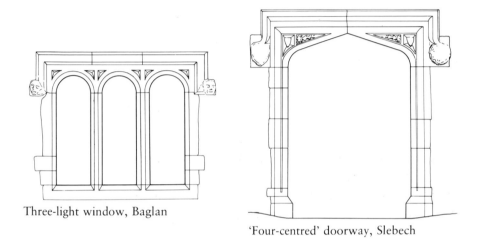

Three-light window, Baglan

'Four-centred' doorway, Slebech

The latest phase of the Gothic style, which lasted until the Reformation. There is more emphasis on the vertical line, with windows being divided up into oblong spaces by long mullions. Tracery is still elaborate, although arches are less pointed. The 'Tudor' style is characterized by flatter arches. Slebech, Tenby chantry and Poynton display good examples of Perpendicular craftsmanship.

ARCHAEOLOGICAL AND ARCHITECTURAL TERMS

AISLE A space parallel to, but divided from, the main body of a church.

APSE The polygonal or rounded end of a chancel or chapel. The remains of an apsidal chancel can be seen at Capel Maelog.

ARCADE A row of arches and pillars separating an aisle from the rest of the church. Good examples can be seen at Llanwarne and Llanidan.

ARCH-BRACE A roof truss with an arched underside formed by the joining of two curved timbers.

AUMBRY A mural recess or cupboard.

BELL-COTE A turret for containing the Sanctus bell.

BUTTRESS A mass of stonework built up against a wall to support or strengthen it.

CHANCEL The eastern end of the church containing the high altar. This part was reserved for the priests and was usually screened from the nave, or demarcated by a raised step and chancel arch.

CHOIR Part of a large church which contains the seats, or stalls, where services were sung or chanted.

FONT A stone basin for containing sacred water used in baptisms. Many fonts are older than the church in which they are found, dating from a previous building on the site. A good example can be seen at Slebech.

GRANGE The outlying estate, or farm, of a monastery, staffed by 'lay brothers'. Such establishments usually had their own chapel, as at Stanton, Margam and Woolaston.

HILL-FORT Hilltop earthworks dating to the Iron Age (*c.* 500 BC–AD 100). The churches of St Mary's at Caerau and St Leonard's at Rudbaxton were built within such prehistoric fortifications.

LANCET A slender window with a plain pointed head.

LYCH-GATE From the Saxon *lych* for corpse, this timber-framed churchyard gate was used by mourners to rest the coffin while awaiting the arrival of the clergy for a burial.

MOTTE AND BAILEY A characteristic Norman castle type, consisting of a mound (motte) crowned with a wooden keep, and an adjoining courtyard (bailey). (A 'ringwork' is a similar earthwork castle consisting of an enclosure lacking a motte.) Examples can be seen next to the churches at Caerau, Penmaen and Urishay.

NAVE The 'people's part of the church'; the main body of the church west of the chancel. The nave is generally larger than the chancel, with a higher roof.

PISCINA A stone basin for washing the sacramental vessels, usually located in the wall beside the altar.

PORCH An external building covering the main entrance the church. Many porches had seats along the sides, and were used as school-rooms.

ROOD-LOFT A timber loft (or beam) over the chancel arch, supporting an image of the crucifixion. Such effigies rarely survived the Reformation, although their existence is often indicated by beam-holes and stairways. The remains of loft stairs can be seen at Newton and Llanfihangel Abercywyn.

TRACERY The decorative stonework in the upper part of a window. In the later Middle Ages this took on very elaborate and intricate patterns.

TRANSEPT A right-angled wing projecting from the nave. Many larger churches, such as Slebech and Llanddwyn, have opposing transepts which form a cruciform plan.

TYMPANUM A large slab infilling the rounded head of a Norman window or door. Many were plain (as at Abberley and Edvin Loach), while others were 'picture books' illustrating religious scenes (e.g. Shobdon).

VAULT An arched stone roof, sometimes with a raised 'rib' moulding. St Govan's chapel and Llawhaden have plain vaults, while St Thomas' chapel at Ludlow has the remains of rib-vaulting.

SOME WELSH TERMS

CAPEL Church or chapel (including Nonconformist buildings).

EGLWYS Church.

FFYNNON Spring or well.

LLAN Church site. The name originates in the 'sacred enclosures' of the Dark Ages.

REFERENCES AND FURTHER READING

JOURNALS AND PERIODICALS

Archaeologia Cambrensis
Archaeology in Wales
Archaeological Journal
Bulletin of the Board of Celtic Studies
Medieval Archaeology
Transactions of the Salop Archaeological Society
Transactions of the Woolhope Society

PUBLISHED WORKS

Buildings of England series Edited by Sir Nikolaus Pevsner (Penguin)
Celtic Church in Wales, The by Sian Victory (SPCK, 1977)
English Parish Church, The by Gerald Randall (Batsford, 1982)
History of Monmouthshire vol. 3 by Sir Joseph Bradney (1923)
Kelly's Directory of Gloucestershire (1897)
Landscape of the Welsh Marches by Trevor Rowley (Michael Joseph, 1986)
Old Parish Churches of Shropshire by Mike Salter (Folly Publications, 1988)
Wales in the Early Middle Ages by Wendy Davies (Leicester University Press, 1982)

ROYAL COMMISSION ON ANCIENT AND HISTORICAL MONUMENTS (RCAHM) PUBLISHED INVENTORIES

Anglesey (1937)
Caernarfonshire (1956–64)
Carmarthenshire (1917)
Denbighshire (1914)
Flintshire (1912)
Herefordshire (1934–36)
Pembrokeshire (1925)

INDEX

Numbers in italic refer to illustrations.